Music Ministry
A Guidebook

donald clark measels, editor

SMYTH&H
PUBLISHING, INCORPORATED

D1472388

Smyth & Helwys Publishing, Inc.
6316 Peake Road
Macon, Georgia 31210-3960
1-800-747-3016

The paper used in this publication meets the minimum requirements of
American National Standard for Information Sciences—
Permanence of Paper for Printed Library Materials.
ANSI Z39.48–1984. (alk. paper)

Library of Congress Cataloging-in-Publication Data

Music ministry : a guidebook /
Donald Clark Measels, editor.
p. cm.
Includes bibliographical references.
ISBN 1-57312-414-1 (alk. paper)
1. Ministers of music.
2. Music in churches.
I. Measels, Donald Clark, 1952-
ML3001 .M86 2003
264' .2—dc21

2003014567

Introduction

This volume is intended as an introduction to church music administration. Several individuals were asked to write one or more chapters about subjects of which they have exceptional knowledge. While this book does not delve into all areas of the music ministry—notable absences include the developing use of electronics and the use of praise bands—it is my hope that readers will gain insight into the work of the leader of the music program.

A note of thanks must be added to the numerous people who helped prepare this book. I wish to make special mention of my wife, Nenette, for assistance with the final editing.

—Donald Clark Measels

Soli Deo Gloria

Contents

Paul B. Clark Jr.

Who Is the Minister of Music?

Have you seen the circus act where the clown spins a series of china plates on flexible sticks braced to the ground? The clown gets one plate spinning, steps to another stick, and sets another plate in motion. Once that plate is rotating at the right speed, he returns to the first to give it another whirl. Then he sets a third plate on another stick and gets it going. He checks the previous two plates and gives them a quick spin if needed to keep them from falling. On it goes, plate after plate, until there may be ten, twelve, or even more plates spinning all at once. There comes a point when the clown dashes madly from plate to plate just to keep them from crashing to the ground. The routine is comical as the clown's wild gestures keep the plates in motion. This is especially true when he tends to a plate at one end of the row and sees a plate losing momentum at the other end. It is sadistically entertaining to feel the tension that mounts as the number of plates increases. The crowd often gasps as they see one of the plates losing centripetal force to the point that collapse appears imminent.

This scenario describes the life of the minister of music. Some of the spinning plates are weekly worship service planning, choir rehearsal preparation, choir member recruitment, lay leader enlistment and training, finance administration, ministerial visitation, and community participation, to name a few. In addition, the music minister has responsibilities and time demands as a member of the church staff team. Add to these and other work-related responsibilities the normal demands of family life, and you begin to sense the tension music ministers face.

The Minister of Music Is a Christian

A Believer

Perhaps the most basic presumption of the minister of music is that he believes in Jesus Christ as his personal Savior. The reason for this presumption would seem obvious: the minister has arrived at an understanding of vocational purpose because of a personal relationship with Christ. It is critical for a minister preparing for vocational service to be certain that faith foundations are clear. The security found in a personal relationship to Christ will play a crucial role in dealing with life and ministry situations. Belief not only refers to centering our thoughts on giving ourselves to God, but also to our faith that God has placed claims upon us. Therefore, we act in response to those claims. In other words, it is not as important that we are "hanging on to Jesus" as that he has hold of us. As a Christian minister, it is important to know that we belong to God and that God has a plan for us as people and as ministers.

A Follower

A Christian is a follower of Jesus Christ. Following Christ in the modern world requires basic disciplines of the Christian faith. Consistent devotional life, prayer, and Bible study seem to be basic elements of following Jesus. Other acts of following grow from these disciplines. One act is that of confession and repentance of sin, which is part of the human condition. The minister must take special care at this point because the pressure to appear "above reproach" can cause her or him to deny the sinful nature and the fundamental need to confess attitudes and actions that do not please God. Pride is an intense temptation for those who minister in roles with a high level of visibility and "performance," as often is the case for the music minister. It is critical for the minister of music to allow close scrutiny of his or her motives by the Holy Spirit, and this is accomplished through Scripture and by being accountable to other Christians.

Some accountability occurs in fellowship with other ministers of music. Denominations and community ecumenical groups provide opportunities for fellowship, spiritual growth, and professional helps through ongoing relationships with others who share similar ministry situations. In many locations, these are formally organized entities. Where that is not the case, the minister of music might begin such a group. Maintaining relationships in these groups takes a level of personal discipline and a servant spirit. Full- and part-time music ministers are involved in nonstop responsibilities within their own congregations. The practice of ongoing participation in music minister fellowship groups must become a priority as a part of personal spiritual practice, discipline, and accountability. As a denominational leader in this area, I have often seen people practice their music ministry as if they lived alone on an island. The result is that they become a lonely brother or sister in need when their ministry situation unravels either due to circumstances of their own making or to circumstances beyond their control. Suddenly, the need for fellowship becomes apparent. Often, portions of their dilemma might have been avoided had they participated in common fellowship with others throughout their ministry days.

The Minister of Music Is a Worshiper

The minister-musician is a worshiper. Over the years, church staff members charged with music leadership have worn different titles. In America, they have been called "song leader," "music director," "minister of music," "music pastor," and "worship leader." Other variations include "choirmaster," "associate pastor/music," and "assistant pastor/worship." The most recent trend has been to include the word "worship" in the title of the minister-musician. This practice implies an emphasis on the responsibility of planning for the corporate worship experience of the congregation. No other responsibility for the minister of music, regardless of title, should be approached with more reverence and humility than this charge of planning the elements of congregational corporate worship.

Personal Worship

A crucial element in planning and leading others in worship is the ongoing practice of personal worship by those who plan. While a single definition of worship eludes us, most attempts at articulating a definition include certain critical elements, such as praise, prayer, confession, and Scripture-reading. Jesus indicated that God looks for worshipers who will worship in "spirit and truth" (John 4:24). In order to stand before others with integrity and invite them into an activity of worship, the worship leader must be engaged in the ongoing practice of personal worship in "spirit and truth." The "truth" aspect of worship implies that this is not a false ritual or an emotionally temporal experience. Rather, it is authentic reverence for an eternal being far greater than us and worthy of our very lives. For the corporate worship leader, this practice must be the essence of position in life. In other words, the practice of personal worship will involve times set aside to be alone with God—praying, singing, listening, reading the word, and confessing our sins. It also involves a never-ending, personal perspective that we live our lives as an act of worship to the Giver of life. The apostle Paul says it well in Romans 12:1-2 (NIV):

> Therefore, I urge you, brothers, in view of God's mercy, to offer your bodies as living sacrifices, holy and pleasing to God—this is your spiritual

act of worship. Do not conform any longer to the pattern of this world, but be transformed by the renewing of your mind. Then you will be able to test and approve what God's will is—his good, pleasing and perfect will.

Corporate Worship

The minister of music is a participant in corporate worship. Whether he or she stands before a gathered body of believers inviting participation in corporate singing, directs a choir or other specialized musical group, or sits in a pew during a portion of the corporate worship service, the minister of music must be a participating worshiper with the body of Christ. While playing a unique role in the service of worship, the minister of music is also a part of the body. When directing the congregation in singing, the minister of music must also sing as a part of that congregation in spirit and, I believe, in auditory blend. If the minister of music is committed to this philosophical position, then care must be taken not to sing over the congregation but to be part of the congregational choir. This implies the absence of constant microphone amplification for the entire length of congregational songs. While the music leader may need to begin a song by leading for a phrase or two, dominating the congregation with amplification throughout the entire song robs the experience of its purest intention. The music leader can even become engrossed in the sound of his or her own voice and become oblivious to the participation level of the congregation, which is counterproductive to the real responsibility of the "worship leader."

I recognize there are other philosophical stances that stem primarily from the contemporary practices of "seeker services" and that genre. The hypothesis in the "seeker" environment is that the attendees are unbelievers and do not know the songs, nor do they believe and therefore cannot sing with enthusiasm even as they catch on. The thinking for "seeker services" has been that the music leader(s) needed amplification to match the popular music style and to be certain that the sound was continuous since the seekers may or may not participate in group singing.

Some of these practices have spilled into common usage in believers' corporate worship without careful attention to sound theological and philosophical basis. The basis for such practices deserves close scrutiny by those who have worship leadership responsibilities, namely pastors and music ministers. Evidence of the diversion from sound philosophical practice can be noted in the inordinate amount of attention given in churches and in "worship conferences" to sound system design and usage without considering its affects on the overall participation of the congregation. Often little attention is given to the congregation's sound—what they can hear of one another, the corporate body gathered in worship.

It is important to share another word of caution in this area. It is easy for one called "worship leader" to draw attention to self. In the attempt to encourage others to worship, the one who has planned and prepared for the participatory response may try to drive the experience or make something happen. There is a clear distinction between emotional manipulation and genuine expression of worship. I believe there is also a difference between personal worship and public worship, especially for the one who stands before the body in the corporate experience. Perhaps the most appropriate approach is to lead corporate worship with humility as a fellow-worshiper, with resolve as one who seeks to offer leadership to the church, and with spiritual dependency, recognizing that true spiritual dynamic occurs only at the bidding of the Holy Spirit of the God whom we worship.

The Minister of Music Is a Servant

The minister of music is a Christian servant. This servant-musician has the grand opportunity to apply the artistry and ministry of musical gifts to the enterprise of serving church, community, and individuals. Jesus called upon his disciples to be "servants of all" (Matt 9:35). The true servant spirit is evident in the way a minister of music leads worship. It is obvious in how others are treated and in what priorities rise to the top among ministry actions and projects. The performance aspect of music ministry can become a stumbling block that would cause the minister of music to become a celebrated performer as soloist or conductor rather than a servant. Training for the musician, regardless of stylistic considerations, always points toward quality performance. The servant-minister-musician must maintain a sacrificial attitude so that the performance quality seeks to draw attention only to the One being praised, rather than to the one(s) performing. People in the choir and the congregation will experience the level of servanthood of the minister of music in the individual relationship they have with the minister, in how they are treated, and in the spiritual emphasis the leader gives during the process of musical preparation. The effective Christian servant patterns life after the servant model of Christ.

The Minister of Music Is a Witness

The Christian minister of music is a witness for Christ. Paul said, "I am not ashamed of the gospel" (Rom 1:16), and that should be the obvious attitude of a minister of music desiring to be an effective Christian in his or her community. Proclamation of the Christian message comes in many forms, and the minister of music has an obvious outlet through the power and drama of music. Fundamentally, though, the minister of music must have a world-consciousness to live a Christian life and to share faith. This is part of what it means to be Christian.

The Minister of Music Is a Church Staff Member

Perhaps no other dimension of the music minister's life can be more gratifying and affirming, or more trouble-riddled and devastating, than relationships with others who serve as ministers on the church staff. Colleagues who serve the same congregation under the Lordship of Christ with an appreciation of each other's gifts and a mutual respect for each other have the opportunity to develop close relationships professionally and personally. Congregations who are privileged to be served and led by staffs demonstrating harmonious relationships are freed to focus on developing their own gifts in ministry actions and Christian service. The model of the church staff in close fellowship shows the church family how to appreciate one another and to expend energy in kingdom work.

Conversely, the church staff embroiled in controversy over philosophical differences, personality clashes, turf protection, and jealousy find themselves living in misery, struggling to be effective as ministers and Christians. This too-common scenario provides the most negative models for a congregation trying to function as the family of God. Congregation members frequently find themselves choosing sides in devotion to one leader or another among the church staff when divisive attitudes prevail. The emotional components of ministry provide the potential for division among church staff. As ministers offer support for families and individuals in need, often a sense of allegiance to the minister providing such service develops. This is not a problem when secure individual ministers share common allegiance to the greater good of the congregation and can celebrate the affirmation that comes through personal ministry relationships. However, when jealousy creeps in to those other than the individual being celebrated, or when pride grows in the one being celebrated, interpersonal troubles often begin. Likewise, when public display of talents draws attention and notoriety to the minister, these same strong forces can damage relationships.

The music minister is particularly susceptible to these dynamics. The performance nature of the musician's function tends to draw attention to talent and personal ability. American culture's appreciation for musical talent adds to the potential for individual notoriety by parishioners. Staff members who do not have opportunity for public display of their abilities can become jealous of the musician and of the pastor, both of whom have consistent exposure. Another potential conflict stemming from these dynamics is a clash between the pastor and the music leader. If one of these receives more acclaim than the other, and either struggles with a sense of personal insecurity, then problems can develop.

Church staffs should spend time evaluating their relationships and encouraging open communication regarding such issues. There are tools available through denominational offices and other entities to assist staffs in evaluating and understanding their working relationships and interpersonal dynamics.

The senior pastor is staff leader in most church staff organizations. The minister of music will do well to appreciate this relationship and spend prayerful energy coming to an understanding of how the senior pastor leads and how the work of the music leader can best support the pastor's ministry of leadership. The particular dynamics of shared leadership in the worship environment deserve close study. In this field of ministry, the greatest potential both for good and for harm exists in the partnership of the pastor and music minister. The wise music minister will expend great effort in communicating with the senior pastor relative to worship service elements. The music minister can help the pastor's sense of security by demonstrating ongoing loyalty to assist the pastor's ministry and to prayerfully link all elements of the worship services together as one event.

Current practice of calling the minister of music the "worship leader" can be problematic in relationship-building as well. While the music leader may be responsible for the bulk of the planning for the worship service experiences, the senior pastor will likely maintain ultimate responsibility for the services. Recognition of the pastor as worship leader in this sense will help the music minister keep an appropriate understanding of this relationship.

The minister of music has a grand opportunity to intersect every area of ministry within the church. Music ministry is not age-specific. Care must be taken by the minister of music to demonstrate avid support for other staff ministers as appropriate. For example, the music minister could volunteer to serve as a sponsor on selected youth trips, where the minister of music is not playing an "up-front" role. This demonstrates support and offers an opportunity to develop personal relationships with students, who may then be invited to participate in a student choir. Parents and fellow ministers will appreciate the music minister's demonstration of concern for the whole student and not just for his or her musical potential.

The Minister of Music Is a Community Member

The minister of music lives and serves as a part of the community. Time demands placed on the minister of music can make it difficult to be active in civic organizations, parent-teacher functions, etc. Determining to be a good neighbor and servant in daily life in the community should be a basic understanding of the lifestyle of every Christian, especially those who represent the church due to their vocational position. Where possible, the music minister should be an active advocate of positive community relations. Participation as a contributing member of the community gives an important witness to the Christian lifestyle—that of caring for individuals as whole people.

A special opportunity for relationship exists for the music minister with local school musicians. Offering assistance to the local high school band or chorus director can pay dividends in developing good will with fellow music leaders, parents, and students, and can pave the way for exchanging resources needed for special programming. Another opportunity for positive community relations may be through participation in community choral/instrumental choirs or bands. There is clear benefit for the local music minister to be recognized as a music leader in the community at many different levels. Opportunities for positive public relations for the church and for personal witness grow out of participation in such groups.

The Minister of Music Is a Family Member

Last, but not least, the minister of music is a family member. After the individual's relationship with Christ, the relationship to spouse, children, parents, and extended family are most critical. The most talented musician who does not have a good home situation will likely be an ineffective minister. Personal integrity is often most clearly demonstrated by the treatment of those who live under the same roof with us. How the minister responds to difficulties at home gives followers a model of to how their own life situations can be handled. Leadership by the minister of music is strengthened or weakened as congregation members observe the respect given by the minister's family and how the minister treats his or her family in public. Words spoken in private to other church members by the spouse and children of the minister of music can make or break the effectiveness of a staff member.

The minister of music who desires to be effective in long-term ministry must take the necessary time to nurture relationships in the home with each member of the family. Many ministers (music and otherwise) have fallen due to inadequate time expenditures at home. Mistreatment or inattention paid to those who live under the same roof will do more to harm a minister's credibility than poor performance in ministerial duties. The responsibility for personal integrity begins at home. The minister of music must be an effective spouse before being able to help others who struggle in that relationship. The father or mother whose children know of their love and proper discipline is able to invite others to follow in Christlike living. Music ministers who help their own children discover the joys of giving thanks and praise to God for life will be free to invite others to join the songs of praise. It is wise for ministers to recognize that their first calling is to be ministers to their own families.

Spin the Plates

There are many plates to spin for the minister of music. They cannot all be spun at once; no one has that many hands. Faith in the One who has called you into this role is necessary to maintain confidence as to which plate most deserves your present attention. The result of trying to fulfill the role of the minister of music apart from this faith is disastrous. Many plates will fall and break into a million pieces. The result of answering the call to serve as music minister, trusting the One who has called us into this awesome responsibility and privilege, offers great reward through the days of this life and into the life to follow.

• *Paul B. Clark Jr. is a Worship Specialist with the Tennessee Baptist Convention and has served as a successful minister of music.*

Donald Clark Measels

Vision, Planning, and Assessment for the Music Ministry

When a new music minister arrives to begin work, it is likely that the person should progress along at least two tracks. It will be important to continue and hopefully improve the day-to-day and week-to-week operation of the program (worship, ensembles, and soloists) while getting to know (and assessing) the music ministry of the new church.

The music minister must also begin strategic, long-range planning. This consideration for the future of the music ministry is my primary focus in this article. The three most important aspects of such a process are developing a vision for what the program can be, planning and working for that outcome, and assessing the success of those labors. After determining how well the plan has worked, adjustments can be made that will better focus goals and plans for the future.

Visioning

Every organization needs a purpose. This is as true for the church as it is for business, families, or institutions. The mission, purpose, or vision tells us what we are about or what we hope to accomplish and provides a concise reference that helps us focus on the most important things. It allows us to begin with the end in mind.

The following are a few examples of mission statements from several religious organizations and churches:

• The purpose of the Executive Board teams of the Arkansas Baptist State Convention is to serve churches and associations as their primary partner in fulfilling the Great Commission. [Their defining documents continue with a vision statement and information on their core values.]

- *The Birmingham Christian Family* exists to provide Christians and the community at large with ways to grow and develop as a part of Birmingham's Christian Family. The local publication is designed to promote positive living by sharing with readers the latest news on entertainment, healthy living, parenting and inspirational literature, as well as what individuals and organizations are doing to try to address the needs of the family.

- The Cooperative Baptist Fellowship is a fellowship of Baptist Christians and churches who share a passion for the Great Commission of Jesus Christ and a commitment to Baptist principles of faith and practice. Our mission: serving Christians and churches as they discover and fulfill their God-given mission.

- The mission of the Irish Bible Institute is to serve the Church through commitment to excellence in Biblical education and leadership development for the Irish Church.

- Coventry Cathedral presents—Our values in worship, mission, and service: openness, excellence and daring—Our core purpose: discovering and celebrating the reconciling love of God—Our goal: to become a world center of pilgrimage, faith-discovery, justice, and reconciliation.

- Our mission at Prestonwood Baptist Church is to glorify God by introducing Jesus Christ as Lord to as many people as possible and develop them in Christian living using the most effective means to impact the world, making a positive difference in this generation.

- The Mission of Second Presbyterian Church is to glorify God through joyful worship, to show God's love to all people, to lead them to faith in Jesus Christ, to make them His disciples, and to call them to His service.

- St Luke's United Methodist Church is an open community of Christians gathering to seek, celebrate, live, and share the love of God for all creation.

Though it has not been formalized into a church mission statement, my pastor emphasizes in his concluding remarks each week that we are a Christian faith community that is together in love, together in loss, and together in labor for the kingdom.

The Bible certainly offers hints as to the mission of the church. Many churches point immediately to the Great Commission: "Then Jesus came to them and said, 'All authority in heaven and on earth has been given to me. Therefore go and make disciples of all nations, baptizing them in the name of the Father and of the Son and of the Holy Spirit, and teaching them to obey everything I have commanded you. And surely I am with you always, to the very end of the age'" (Matt 28:18-20). Matthew 22:36-39 expands the Great Commission: "'Teacher, which is the greatest commandment in the Law?' Jesus replied: 'Love the Lord your God with all your heart and with all your soul and with all your mind. This is the first and greatest commandment. And the second is like it: Love your neighbor as yourself.'"

There is no one mission declaration that will work for every church simply because each church circumstance is different. For instance, a church that is adjacent to a college may emphasize ministry to college students. Whatever the church situation, the mission must in its essence speak to glorifying God and edifying the saints.

It is the responsibility of the music ministry to fit within the mission of the church, and any purpose statements should reflect that position. The music ministry mission should be the musical reflection of the purpose agreed to by the church. Vision must be developed under the leadership of the Holy Spirit and must have broad understanding and support by the people in the music ministry, the staff, and the church as a whole. Although the talents and interest of the music minister are factors, visioning is not simply an opportunity to gain formal recognition of favorite programs, styles, or approaches.

The best way to develop broad support is to use a participatory process to develop any defining vision documents. This may take time. If statements are already in place, the music minister might decide to have meetings with various constituents as to the relevance and viability of that mission.

Planning

When the music ministry has agreed to a statement of purpose, it is time to decide on a plan. Music ministry plans need to be developed with strong participation by interested church members and leaders. Always remember that congregants will be a major part of the program, and music ministry programs must be coordinated with the plans of other staff members and lay church leaders. It is always better to collaborate than to have each program of the church going in its own potentially contradictory direction.

In the process of developing a plan for the music ministry, there are a number of factors to consider. The size and age demographics of the church and community may give direction. For instance, there is little possibility for a youth choir if there are few people in the youth Sunday school departments.

Some knowledge of the music programs of the local school systems and the ministries of other local churches is essential. However, I once heard a successful music minister say that we cannot expect others to train the people needed for the church program to be successful. The lesson is that if we want a singing church, or have the need for more keyboard players, or need violins for the church orchestra, then we should set about training/preparing those people for service.

The financial situation of the church and the approved budget for the music ministry are important guides. It is not wise to project an expensive ministry if adequate financial resources are not likely to be available. Staff, talent, and willing workers will dictate the size and types of ministry that can be implemented and led by people other than the music minister. In addition, the size and content of the music library, the potential for recruiting, and the program history of the ministry have important implications for planning and future success.

After collecting information, the music minister and an appropriate group of advisors can begin the process of strategic planning for the music ministry. The advisory group must include key ensemble and program leaders and should incorporate the music committee of the church, if one exists. It may be that an annual "Music Ministry Summit" for planning and evaluation should be held. If there is an annual meeting, it should be conducted after most programs have finished meeting for the year and before planning and re-staffing for fall programs begins. Budget preparation for the church at large may not easily complement the timing of the music ministry planning and evaluation meeting. At my church, the budget year begins on the first of April, but the perception is that the music ministry year begins with the start of the fall music groups. The music ministry must accommodate the budget process and time line of the church.

The Plan

Most plans will involve large, long-range goals, intermediate steps that need to be accomplished in order to reach those long-range goals, and daily tasks that must be accomplished so the intermediate steps can be realized.

One example might be:

Long-range Goal
Develop a graded handbell program

Intermediate Steps
Build support for the program (ministers, finance committee, prospective leaders and players, church at large)
Find funding for the purchase of bells and equipment
Discover a location for the bells to be stored and to rehearse

Daily Tasks
Purchase bells, equipment, music
Schedule rehearsals and performances
Recruit the groups or replacements
Set up the bells and the rehearsal room
Plan the rehearsals, mark the music, assign the bells

Once there is a plan, the intermediate steps and daily tasks must be accomplished. As the old saying goes: "Plan your work and work your plan."

Assessment

Once the long-range goals, intermediate steps, and daily tasks are in place and the work is being done or is complete, there must be ways of evaluating the plan. Each program or group should be evaluated by the goals set for that group and the mission statement of the music ministry and the church. The music minister should make periodic assessments as to the progress made in each area. These occasional evaluations may give early indications of difficulties in a given program and will offer the music minister the opportunity to take action if necessary. Praise and appreciation can be given to the participants and volunteer leaders who make the program work. However, if it is discovered, for example, that one children's choir worker exercises corporal punishment during rehearsals, the music minister has much to consider and potentially difficult actions to take.

On an annual basis, a more detailed evaluation should take place and may be part of the "Music Ministry Summit." Simple things, like enrollment and attendance, will give indications of success or problems. Certainly, the performance of each individual group is one of the strongest markers. Evaluations should not be an excuse for severe criticism of specific individuals. The process should be dominantly positive and focused on enhancing the effectiveness of the program. Always attempt to be both honest and caring.

Among the resources a music minister might consult for further information are the numerous volumes on planning found in the business section of a good bookstore. The materials available from Franklin Covey on the web, in their retail stores, and through their seminars are also helpful.

I encourage you to enter into strategic planning in your ministry. May God help us see what we can become, be diligent workers that glorify him, and help others.

• **Donald Clark Measels** *is the Dean of Fine Arts at Carson-Newman College in Jefferson City, Tennessee, where he teaches church music.*

Donald Clark Measels

The Calendar and the Minister of Music

The ideal way for a music minister to coordinate church music is for the pastor to provide sermon topics and Scripture readings months in advance of any given Sunday. My new pastor made available six months of sermon titles, Scriptures, and theme developments before he arrived to begin his ministry. That information gave me the opportunity to plan intentionally choir anthems and other portions of the service. Many pastors follow the church year and the common lectionary. Thus, the music minister has the opportunity to know years in advance the Scripture readings for any Sunday. Hopefully, it will be possible to collaborate with your pastor far enough in advance of the services to prepare appropriate music.

It might be helpful to begin by rehearsing the purpose for worship. Harold Best says, "Worship is the creator loving the creation and the creation loving the creator."[1] This rhetorical approach to a definition gives wide latitude and speaks of appreciation, admonition, and communication. It might also be helpful to remember Søren Kierkegaard's model for worship, especially in our entertainment-oriented world. Kierkegaard imagines us in a theatrical setting where worship leaders are prompters, members of the congregation are actors, and God is the audience.[2] The only problem with this analogy is that God is more active and responsive in worship than Kierkegaard may have allowed. The idea is to point the attention of the congregation to God, to God's love for us, and to our sins in comparison to God's perfection, and then try not to distract the actors/the congregants.

Worship is the most important activity of the church, and even congregations in the "free church" tradition follow some annual pattern of activities. Each church has its own unique mixture of important days that originate in the historical church year, denominational emphases, local interest and tradition, and patriotic celebrations. In addition to information about the pastor's plans, it is essential for the minister of music to have a clear understanding of what the church expects on each of those days. Only with that information can appropriate plans be made.

Surprising as it may be, 150 years ago most Baptists did not celebrate Christmas, and Easter was the most important Sunday in the church year. For most Baptist churches, the year of Sundays had no real pattern of special days. Now, most of us at least celebrate Christmas and Easter. It is not unusual for Baptists to have several Advent services and perhaps to remember additional days that are the outgrowth of more liturgical churches. This has obvious implications for worship services. We must ask, how do we love God in worship by using the calendar?

The word *liturgy* usually refers to the formal public rituals of religion. Among Protestants, the term has overtones of a fixed form of worship, in contrast to free or spontaneous approaches. Baptists are a diverse people with a wide variety of worship planning and practice. We all perform greeting and parting rituals. Baptist churches are autonomous. They believe and do what the Bible, under the influence of the Holy Spirit, leads them to do. Therefore, no outside agency has the authority to insist on a specific daily or yearly pattern of worship. Each church has the right to "do its own thing."

My contention is that most of us are operationally liturgical; each Sunday we repeat the same actions usually in the same order, and in each year there are congregational expectations regarding special days. To think on a large scale, there are Sundays every year that the membership of your church anticipates will carry a specific theme. Christmas, missions emphases, and Christian Citizenship Sunday might serve as examples. Not every church follows the same pattern. However, this is the norm, not the exception, and perhaps even more so in our smaller churches, where resources and the idea pool may be less broad.

Currently, I serve as a guest minister of music. On a recent Sunday, I asked the congregation to sing a different song in place of the Doxology, which in this church always follows the offertory music. One of the choir members made an impassioned plea for me never to do that again. In no uncertain terms, she strongly stated her preference for singing the Doxology every Sunday. To quote her, "It's the only thing left that's part of my Baptist heritage!" In the words of Tevye of *Fiddler on the Roof,* "Tradition!"

The congregation cooperated with my request to sing a different song on that day, but I was made aware that there were others who would be much more comfortable if I "left their Doxology alone." When I changed the location of the anthem in the service order, the church secretary called to say I had made a mistake.

In your church, it may not be the Doxology, the Lord's Prayer, or the placement of the special music, but there are traditions unique to each church that some members feel should remain unaltered. The minister of music must know in advance about these practices. That is not to say that he or she will continue these bits of Baptist liturgy, but any changes should be planned, and the congregation should be prepared to expect them.

The Church Year

Some psychologists use a continuum with "autonomy" as one pole and "connectedness" as the other pole when they try to describe aspects of a personality. There is some application to churches and denominations as well. Typically, from their birth Baptist churches have wanted to remain independent. Little need was felt for connection to other churches. Basically, the first Baptists fled a smothering, controlling parent, and the denomination for centuries only slightly moderated its desire for separation from other groups and hierarchies. With considerable controversy, associations and conventions eventually developed. Many practices of the smothering, controlling parent have remained difficult for Baptists to embrace.

In any such situation, there is the danger of discarding some good with the bad—the proverbial "baby out with the bath water" idea. One of the areas where we have been too hasty or too intense in our rejection of the "establishment" is our unwillingness to consider the use of a Christian church year and lectionary. These two areas of interest are grand in concept and important enough that we should consider them.

Baptists are known as free-church Christians, and most claim they do not follow the church year. However, we do observe a church year of sorts. Use the following questions to examine the use of the calendar by your church. Does your church celebrate Christmas? Does it use a service to talk about the New Year? In February around Valentine's Day, does your church have services based on "love"? Before Easter, is Palm Sunday mentioned and do you celebrate Easter? In May, does your church have a service that emphasizes Memorial Day? How about the Sunday before July Fourth?

Recently, the students in one of my classes talked about the dates usually observed in their churches each year. The list included Christmas and Easter, Mother's Day, Father's Day, graduation recognition, Memorial Day, the Fourth of July, Thanksgiving, missions Sundays, revivals, and baby dedication. There was the possibility of additional days with worship implications including the Super Bowl, sports teams recognition, fall festivals, etc. The Baptist church year indicates few influences from the life of Christ and many more events or seasons that are the result of cultural, national, denominational, and local church pressures.

Most of us do not consider this an aberration. We remember these special days every year in our services. Most Baptist churches will include, more or less, these items and other dates as special emphases depending on the traditions of the local church and the decisions of the current pastor. Even Baptist churches have traditions that rise to the level of a "Church Year" or an annual series of services set aside for special themes. The minister of music has the opportunity to change or at least adapt this situation. The practices of the local church must be clearly understood and evaluated. The question must be asked about each service, "Is this the right thing for a church to do?" Plans must be made accordingly.

The start of the church year is not January. In fact, it begins with what is known as the season of Advent, which usually starts in late November. Advent is followed by the festival of Christmas beginning on Christmas Day and lasting twelve days. Then there is Epiphany, which deals with Jesus' ministry and the light he brought to our world. Lent, which begins during February on Ash Wednesday, is the time when we anticipate Christ's sacrifice on Good Friday. Sometimes fasting or another type of sacrifice is involved.

My introduction to Lent occurred when my seminary pastor and his family were hosting an exchange student for a semester. The young high school girl was Catholic, and when Lent arrived she gave up the enjoyment of chocolate and Coca-Cola®. The intent was to help her relate to the idea of sacrifice.

The most important celebration of the Christian year is Easter. Though we tend to celebrate it for only one day, in the more liturgical church Easter extends for several weeks and includes the ascension of Jesus into heaven. The season of Easter is succeeded by Pentecost, which celebrates the beginning of the church.

For the purposes of this article, only the seasons of the church year that are most directly related to the life of Christ have been included. There are a number of other dates and season that could be celebrated, but these seem to be the most significant.

All churches big and small should reexamine their opportunities to change lives through a planned, macro, or yearlong vision of emphases. There is a purer way to progress than most of us have used, and a Baptist adaptation of a liturgical calendar could be a healthy revival for our churches.

We should at least give more thought to the life of Christ, including those periods of the year known as Advent, Christmas, and Epiphany. These are literally periods in which the church focuses attention on proclaiming that Christ is the light of the world. Then there are the times referred to as Lent, Easter, and Pentecost. During this time, the church is asked to pay special attention to the death, resurrection, and ascension of Jesus the Christ and the coming of the Holy Spirit. If the metaphorical smothering parent still frightens us, we do not need to use the terms, but the concepts are good.

Remember, as ministers, it is our job to aid worship—the creation loving the creator and the creator loving the creation—and not to distract worshipers. There are a number of distractions in our current practice.

What are we saying to our congregations by the special days we celebrate each year? What should we be saying? Do we need to make changes?

Using a Lectionary

Baptists are known as "People of the Book," that is, the Bible. However, if we consider the amount of Scripture read in the average Baptist service, we would not immediately come to that conclusion. We must have gotten that reputation because of our strong Sunday school, Bible drill programs, and winter Bible studies. Most of the Baptist services I have attended included only the Scripture on which the preacher based the sermon.

One of the best traditions any church could start would be the systematic reading of Scripture in their worship services. Those readings could be drawn from a variety of sources. A three-year cycle of Scripture readings is readily available for use. It is known as the lectionary. One of the best things about this method is that these readings are chosen to follow the church year. There are several denominationally-based versions from which to choose. After the three-year cycle of reading these Scriptures each Sunday, the congregation will have heard a major portion of the Bible. If the talk is "People of the Book," we should try to "walk the walk."

Another reason to use this method is the large number of available resources based on these readings. One of the most convenient is the web site <www.textweek.com>. The readings for any Sunday can easily be accessed, and there are multiple links to other pages for additional information, including a subscription link that provides sermon aids and a list of hymns that fit the Scriptures. There are also many resources that provide additional appropriate materials for use in the bulletin and for presentation as a part of the service.

The lectionary is also a disciplining agent. I once heard a Baptist pastor in Mississippi indicate that if the lectionary had not required a certain passage to be read, he would never have planned to tackle that Scripture as the basis of a sermon. The use of a lectionary broadened that pastor's cannon of text, broke him out of his comfort zone, and helped him grow through the experience. Scripture should help us grow and move us beyond that to which we are accustomed.

Certainly, there are other ways. A pastor could adopt the practice of having the Sunday school Scripture read each Sunday and using that as the basis for the sermon. However, there is always the risk of other teachers presenting it better than the pastor or, at least, stealing a bit of the thunder.

Perhaps the church leaders would like to prepare their own series of Scriptures. That would be meaningful but time-consuming.

The Scripture offered in the lectionary every Sunday does not always speak to the most important things in the life of a given church. Pastors need the flexibility of being able to follow the Holy Spirit's leadership. A pastor must use the good judgment to minister to the grieving or speak to an unexpected crisis.

Resources about frequently observed events are generally available from the publishing agencies of each denomination. If more information is needed about liturgy and the lectionary, check the publications available from denominations that normally use those materials.

Obviously, the music minister needs to know well in advance what the pastor of the church intends for any given service. If the pastor follows the lectionary, then the music minister has possibilities. If the pastor provides information for services that are eight or more weeks in the future, the music minister has the chance to be thoughtful in selections and to have the musicians prepared. At the least, the music minister needs to know the congregation's expectations for all "special" services and be prepared to deliver or adapt as needed. We should help our congregations love the Creator and not distract them.

• **Donald Clark Measels** *is Dean of Fine Arts at Carson-Newman College in Jefferson City, Tennessee, where he teaches church music.*

NOTES

[1] From a lecture given by Harold Best at a conference on worship for Tennessee Baptist in Brentwood, TN, in 1999.

[2] Donald P. Hustad, *Jubilate II* (Carol Stream, IL: Hope Publishing Company, 1989), 106.

Gene Wilder

What Do Pastors Expect from Music Ministers?

Recently I was talking to a pastor friend who said, "Of all the challenges I face in the ministry, nothing is more exhausting than dealing with ministers of music. Every one I have met is as temperamental as a mother grizzly with cubs and a toothache. I have probably lost more sleep over conflicts with my music minister than all other problems combined!"

Then there is the other side. A music minister stated, "My pastor has no concept of music ministry. During Sunday morning worship he reads his sermon notes while the choir sings the anthem and refers to the offertory as 'filler.' It is awfully hard to work with someone who considers music ministry as nothing more than window dressing for his 'holy orations.'"

Unfortunately, these conflicting scenarios are common. Instead of working together as a staff team, too many music ministers and pastors view themselves as staff competitors. This is unfortunate because few tensions create a more hostile atmosphere within a church than conflicts between a pastor and the minister of music. When such tensions occur, everybody loses.

I was first a music minister; now I am a pastor. Having served in both positions has given me a unique perspective. Hopefully, my perspective can provide insight into establishing ministerial relationships that are not only effective but also fulfilling.

Before discussing a pastor's expectations, let me interject a note of caution for music ministers. Your ministerial effectiveness and your joy in ministry will be greatly affected by the pastor with whom you serve. When considering a staff position, make sure the pastor's worship philosophy and administrative style are complementary to yours. The most heavenly position can quickly become a ministerial hell if you cannot get along with the pastor. Remember, if the music minister and pastor go to war, the music minister is usually the first to taste defeat. So be careful. In searching for a place to serve, the old adage is certainly true—look before you leap!

What do I, as a pastor, expect of a music minister? I expect music ministers to be team players who genuinely care for the people they serve and the people with whom they serve. They should command respect because of their integrity and should be valued because of their professionalism and diligence.

The Music Minister as a Person

While skill, experience, and education are important attributes for ministers of music, they are not the most important attributes. Job performance, even from the most talented individuals, cannot compensate for a minister's lack of genuine care. I have seen minimally talented musicians make excellent music ministers because they genuinely love the people they serve.

Effective music ministers must be genuinely caring people. By its very nature, ministry is a calling to care. The best ministers of music I know see themselves first as ministers and secondly as musicians. They see music as a tool for ministry instead of seeing ministry as an avenue for demonstrating their musicianship.

Because the music ministry is a caring ministry, I expect music ministers to demonstrate their compassion in nonmusical ways. The music minister should be ready to offer help and comfort whenever a crisis arises in the life of a church member, particularly when that member is involved in the church's music ministry. As a music minister your obligation to the congregation does not end when the last note is sung or when the last chord is played.

Members of the congregation will instinctively know whether or not you genuinely care for them. If they sense you do not care, your ministry will not be taken seriously. If they sense your caring spirit, they will empower you to succeed regardless of your musical weaknesses. In ministry, what you do is never more significant than who you are. This is also true in your personal life. Some professionals have the luxury of leaving their job when they leave the office. You will not have such a luxury because your calling to minister is a calling that pervades every part of your life. Like it or not, your business dealings, your family life, and even your recreational activities will be scrutinized by the people you serve. When ministers fail, they fail more quickly from flaws related to their character than from flaws related to job performance.

Because personal integrity and character are so significant, I expect any minister who serves with me to have an exemplary lifestyle. I do not expect perfection, but I do expect them to lead the kind of lives that church members should emulate. I expect them to treasure their families and to stay attentive to the needs of their families. Obviously, ministers will not be perfect husbands and wives, nor will they parent perfect children, but they need to be diligent in their efforts. Work hard to insure that your family relationships remain healthy, for when a minister's family life tumbles, the career is not far behind.

When I begin a search for a minister, I pay close attention to the minister's spouse. While I do not expect the spouse to be an "unpaid bonus," I do look for ministers whose spouses are supportive, caring, and happily involved in the life of the church. Some ministers have spouses who are their greatest asset. Other ministers have spouses who are their greatest liability. You can almost measure the potential success of a prospective staff member by measuring the support of that minister's spouse.

While family issues are paramount to a minister's character, financial management issues are not far behind. Ministers must live within their means. If they do not, their lack of integrity will be the cause of their downfall.

Many search committees ask permission to examine a minister's credit history prior to securing that minister. It is an idea with much merit given the number of ministers who have embarrassed their churches by failing to meet financial obligations. A candidate's credit history speaks volumes about that candidate's integrity. Ultimately, the way we handle our money makes a statement about the way we live our lives, and the way we live our lives is the ultimate declaration of the way we practice our faith.

The Music Minister as a Professional

Warmly professional. That's the term I use when describing my expectation of a minister. By professional, I mean a skilled practitioner who meets or exceeds the accepted standards of a given profession. Like lawyers, physicians, and financiers, music ministers should exude an air of competence in their field, but the air they exude should be "warm" air. There is no place in the ministry for cold professionals who convey their professionalism through aloofness or detachment. Effective ministers of music are approachable and friendly experts. They are knowledgeable artisans who compassionately handle the demands of their calling.

This kind of professional competence is always a product of education and experience. That is why these two items should be prominently displayed on a minister's resume. When I look for a minister of music, I look not only for a person who has significant past education, but for a professional who understands the value of continuing education. In an ever-changing world, competent professionals know the importance of updating their skills and staying abreast of new developments.

There is a personal aspect of professionalism that should not be ignored. A minister's personal appearance makes a statement about professionalism. Grooming and dress are no small issues. They often make statements about us that are louder than the statements we make about ourselves.

Appropriate dress always depends on the community we serve. What is entirely appropriate in one location may be completely inappropriate in another. Some communities expect ministers to dress formally. Others accept less formal attire. Being "overdressed" can be as problematic as being "underdressed." You would do well to take your cues by noticing the wardrobe of other professionals in your congregation.

Like it or not, our work environment tells others much about our professionalism. If I walk into the office of a minister and have to move books and papers to sit down, I begin to question that minister's organizational abilities. For me, clutter is never a sign of busyness or importance. It is an indicator of one's inability to manage work and time.

Punctuality and accountability are also marks of the effective professional. Professionals know the value of time and they respect the schedules of others. They make themselves accountable to those they serve. Pastors and church members rightly question a minister's professionalism when that person is habitually late or when the minister cannot be found during regular working hours.

The other day I tried to call another minister. When his secretary told me he was unavailable, I asked if she could indicate a time to call again. She replied, "I am sorry. I do not know where he is and have no idea when he is coming back." Her reply quickly let me know that either the minister (or his secretary) was something less than a professional.

Let me conclude this section on professionalism by saying a word about "temperamental musicians." More than a few music ministers have gotten a reputation for being temperamental. Unfortunately, some believe being temperamental is simply intrinsic to professional musicians. I believe it is a sign of childish immaturity and can destroy the unity within a staff. No one enjoys walking on eggshells to avoid upsetting a temperamental musician. That is why, as a pastor, I look for music ministers who have enough maturity and professionalism to keep their temperamentalism in check.

The Music Minister as a Member of the Staff Team

A winning baseball team provides a fitting paradigm for the effective church staff. Winning baseball teams consist of many players with diverse individual skills. No player, regardless of his or her skill, can win alone. Winning necessitates the coordinated effort of all team members. Each member of the team has an assigned position and takes responsibility for playing that position to the best of his or her ability. Sometimes a player must move out of position to assist another player. When this is done successfully, neither player feels intimidated or undermined by the other.

Baseball team members must communicate with each other at all times. Each player needs to understand what the other players are doing. A winning team is filled with players who support each other, respect each other, and encourage each other to be the best they can be.

An effective church staff is not unlike a winning baseball team. The church staff is made up of many ministers with diverse individual skills. No minister, regardless of skill, can effectively function alone. Effective ministry is a team effort. Each staff member has an assigned position and serves that position responsibly. Sometimes a staff member must move out of position and assist another staff member. When these changes occur, neither minister should feel intimidated or undermined.

As the church staff works together, communication is vital. Each staff member needs to understand what other staff members are doing. Church staffs are effective when the members of the staff support, respect, and encourage each other to be the best they can be.

I look for an individual who knows how to be a team player. Obviously, a minister's talent is important, but it is not nearly as important as his or her spirit of cooperation.

What does it take to be a team player? First, you must understand the value of accommodation. Ministers who understand the team concept realize that their area of ministry is only one piece of the puzzle. Music ministers are specialists by calling and training, but their job is not to elevate their area of specialization. Their job is not to draw attention to music at the exclusion of other ministries. Their job is to integrate music into all areas of ministry.

In his book on church staff relationships, Herman Sweet warns that an overemphasis on specialization in ministry creates serious dangers for the church. A church staff will not function effectively as a team until all staff members appreciate the interrelationship of their staff position with every other staff position.[1] The job of the second baseman in baseball is not to draw the team's attention to second base. The job is to play the position well so that the entire team can function together.

The same is true with a minister of music. The minister's job is not to draw the church's attention to the ministry of music. Instead, the minister's job is to integrate music into all areas of ministry so the entire ministry team can function together. To integrate your work into the staff team's larger effort, you must be willing to accommodate. Sometimes you will have to alter a rehearsal schedule to accommodate another church function. Sometimes your budget request will be denied so funds can be allocated to another area of ministry. No team can work effectively until each member of that team is willing to accommodate the needs of another.

I recently watched a music minister disassemble the entire set of a Christmas musical to accommodate a funeral service in the sanctuary. While that act was troublesome, it was necessary for the sake of the team. Ministers who are true team players appreciate the importance of accommodation.

Flexibility is also a prerequisite for ministers who want to be part of an effective staff team. The best ministers of music are those who plan their work in advance but who are flexible enough to make last-minute changes. Because of the dynamic nature of ministry, advanced plans often give way to quick changes. The pastor may change the direction of worship and give a two-day notice. A soloist may cancel an hour before the service. Even the best-laid plans are subject to change. Mature ministers learn to cope with these changes without letting the changes affect their attitude. Ministers who are real team players learn the art of flexibility.

A staff team is no more effective than the communication that takes place among team members. Communication is the key to coordinating the many programs of the church. When communication is lacking, chaos is certain. Jerry Brown writes, "Clogged-up communications lines between staff members contribute to all kinds of relational problems such as distancing, power struggles, jealousy, and lack of understanding of one another and his work. A lack of open communication eventually sets up fight or flight patterns of behavior. Most staff problems come from a breakdown in talking with one another."[2]

Effective staff teams communicate in both formal and informal settings, but regardless of the setting, they make open and real communication a priority. Gary Cook writes, "Church staff teams that stay together cultivate an openness in communication. They communicate mainly face-to-face, not by memo or telephone. They sometimes agree to disagree but continue to try to talk themselves together. They talk in the automobile on the way to mutual appointments. They talk on the golf course and tennis court. They talk formally and regularly in staff meetings. They talk to each other, not about each other."[3]

Some communication is informational; other communication is confrontational. Both are vital to the effectiveness of a healthy church staff. Ministers do not always agree and at times that disagreement can create tension within the staff team. Staff members need to talk through issues of conflict until they are resolved. Issues that are never confronted often fester until they become issues that damage the unity of the staff and ultimately the health of the church.

Perhaps the most important ingredient in maintaining staff unity is "respect." I respect the members of my staff and I expect them to return that respect to me. I try to respect their business and personal schedules and I expect them to respect mine. I respect their special gifts and talents and I hope they respect mine. I wholeheartedly affirm Gary Cook's remarks as he writes, "A church staff in a very real sense ought to be a mutual admiration society. This does not imply a constant bragging on each other in front of church members, but it does mean an appreciation of each staff member. It means thankfulness for each other's gifts. It means an affirming awareness of the individual pilgrimage of each member. It means an encouragement to continue in the journey of faith."[4]

The Music Minister as a Worship Leader

Of all the tasks assigned to a music minister, none is more significant than worship planning and leadership. The best ministers of music I have known are those who spend as much time planning music as they do rehearsing and performing. Meaningful worship with consistent quality requires a regular, prayerful, creative dialogue between the pastor, the music minister, and the other church musicians.

One of the most important traits of a good worship planner is the ability to construct meaningful worship experiences that are applicable to the congregations they serve. Each congregation is unique, and that uniqueness should be foremost in the minds of ministers who plan worship. It is not the music minister's job to persuade the congregation to appreciate music the minister appreciates. The task of the worship planner is to choose genres and activities that will most effectively lead the worshiper to experience the presence of God and to respond to the call of God. Some congregations best relate to music that is traditional, if not classical. Other congregations relate best to music that is more contemporary. It is not the job of the music minister to convert the classical congregation into lovers of contemporary music or vice versa. It is the minister's job to find the genre that best relates to the congregation and to use that genre to bring people into the presence of God.

Let me encourage music ministers to help congregations expand their musical horizons. There is nothing wrong with helping the congregation gain an appreciation for a genre that may not be a part of their tradition or background. In fact, the novelty of new forms often adds meaning to the worship experience. Still, new forms should be added cautiously because even the most open congregations resist change.

While in seminary, I was minister of music in a small, rural Texas town. The entire community was enamored with country and western music. Personally, country and western is not my cup of tea. When I first walked into the choir loft, I noticed an ample supply of well-used country western hymnals. Despite my aversion to country and western music, I often incorporated selections from those hymnals in our worship. I did so not because I liked them; I used them because they best related to the congregation I served.

Many congregations today are eclectic. Their musical tastes cover the entire spectrum of musical genres. In these congregations, the minister's task is formidable but not impossible. If proper time and energy are given to planning, musical genres can be combined and blended so the worship experience will relate to as many people as possible.

Another important element in worship planning is creativity. People tend to ignore the familiar. When this week's worship is simply a duplicate of last week's experience, the congregation becomes bored. I value the music minister who devises creative new ways of conveying ancient truths.

Collaboration and cooperation between the pastor and music minister are imperative in order to plan meaningful worship. The theme reflected in the pastor's sermon should be supported and augmented by everything else that happens during that service of worship. This is only possible when both ministers know the theme of the worship. As a pastor, I try to select worship themes and sermon topics six months in advance. This gives my minister of music time to select and purchase music and to explore creative ways of supporting the theme. Unfortunately, your ability to support the worship theme will often depend upon the cooperation and advanced planning of your pastor.

One last element in worship planning that should not be ignored is the element of timing. Worship should be planned to fit the allotted time frame. Few things are more frustrating than to begin one's sermon with the realization that the service is already running too long. As a minister of music, you will quickly create a troublesome relationship with your pastor if you do not honor the limits of time.

Worship planning is important, but the music minister's performance during worship will ultimately enhance or detract from the worship that was planned. From decorum on the platform to the manner of conducting hymns, the music minister's performance makes a difference in worship.

As I have watched music ministers lead worship over the years, I have noticed two common mistakes. First, ministers sometimes become so preoccupied with their role that they ignore or appear disinterested in the roles of others. This mistake is as common with pastors as it is with ministers of music. I have seen pastors reviewing their sermon notes, oblivious to the anthem being sung by the choir. I have also seen choral directors so preoccupied with their upcoming anthem that they ignore the reading of Scripture or a pastoral prayer. Not only is this rude, but it is distracting to other worshipers and diminishes the effectiveness of the entire worship experience.

Another common mistake made by musicians relates to their spoken words from the pulpit. Brief hymn introductions can be effective, but brevity must be underscored. When a music leader preaches a mini-sermon before a hymn, the rhythm of worship is interrupted and the congregation loses attention. Preachers are not usually effective when they "chase rabbits" during their sermons. The same truth applies to ministers of music.

Conclusion

Over the years, I have greatly valued the relationship I have shared with ministers of music. These gifted ministers are vital to the work of the church and to the worship of God. As a pastor, I view them as equals. They do not simply provide window-dressing for my sermons, but their gifts communicate messages my words cannot convey.

In the best situations, the music minister and I have viewed ourselves as uniquely gifted players, called by God to play on the same team, and when we have taken our relationship seriously, we have enjoyed celebrating the thrill of being members of a winning team.

• **Gene Wilder** *is the Pastor of First Baptist Church in Jefferson City, Tennessee.*

NOTES

[1] Herman J. Sweet, *The Multiple Staff in the Local Church* (Philadelphia: Westminster, 1963), 21.

[2] Jerry W. Brown, *Church Staff Teams That Win* (Nashville: Convention Press, 1979), 84.

[3] Gary W. Cook, "Church Staff Working Together in Ministry," *Shared Ministry, A Journey Toward Togetherness in Ministry,* ed. Joe R. Stacker and Bruce Grubbs (Nashville: Convention Press, 1985), 81.

[4] Ibid., 80.

Bo Prosser

Church Staff Relationships

"The church is becoming what the church staff is!"[1]

This statement bears out the importance of positive church staff relationships. There may be no greater challenge facing ministers today than maintaining positive staff relationships with colleagues. If the church of today is going to enjoy a healthy congregational life, the church staff must learn how to relate positively with one another.

The average church has about 90 adults attending each Sunday.[2] This figure will yield approximately 120 to 150 in total attendance each week. The church with 150 in weekly attendance will normally have 2 and maybe 3 staff ministers plus support staff. Even in churches with less than 100 in attendance, there may be multiple staffs sharing in ministry. In churches with only a pastor on staff, there are still staff issues. Although paid staffs of churches vary in size and in issues, the work of any staff is to support and sustain the work and ministry of the church. The staff has a huge responsibility to lead the church. In order to lead effectively, the staff must pay attention to their relationships with one another. Knowing how to hire, blend, and lead is crucial for growing a staff. We cannot do ministry by ourselves.

Most of us want to serve on a well-managed staff. We want to be part of a team of colleagues who share mutual respect and support. The challenge of maintaining high staff morale and unity is one that takes work and insight. The level at which the staff is motivated, dedicated, and forward-thinking will also determine the level at which the church will function.

How do church staffs operate at these high levels of quality and dedication? What needs to happen for staff ministers to form a quality functioning team? How does a senior pastor build respect and unity among staff ministers? How do staff ministers develop a sense of worth and importance?

These are complex questions and so are the answers. The staff is to work together, not as two sides in a tug-of-war or in a master-slave relationship. The hierarchical model must be abandoned in favor of a team approach.

The staff should move in the same direction, working toward the same goals. The staff is to share both the sorrows and the joys of ministering to their congregation.

Five Rules for Relating to the Pastor

The key to staff relationships is the pastor. Regardless of the mind-set, personality, or leadership style of the pastor, staff relationships will hinge on him or her. There are a variety of staff leadership models, but none of these can be put into place without the agreement and support of the pastor. This statement is not to put undue emphasis on the position and role of the pastor. This is certainly not to suggest that the pastor is the only leader on a staff team. However, the pastor is the one to whom everyone looks for direction and leadership. If the above statement is disagreeable, you might want to reexamine your philosophy of church leadership.

Examine the history of your local church. The local congregation divides its history according to the pastors who have served it! The local congregation refers to significant points of its life in terms of the pastor who was leading at the time. Think of your own baptism. Usually, we remember even our baptism in terms of the pastor who baptized us. Rarely do we remember the associates who worked the same hours (or more) to help the church grow and succeed. That is not to say that the associates are unimportant to the work of the church, but rarely has any church included their staff ministers among the pastoral pictures in the hallway. We would do well as staff ministers never to forget that the role of pastor is the "centerpiece" of the staff.

While most pastors are aware of the centrality of their roles, the ways they deal with this "power and authority" vary distinctly. Current leadership literature suggests that the pastor be a visionary leader, coaching the congregation, rallying unselfish giving, and managing the politics of the church. Different pastors approach these roles differently. Some rely upon their egos and the power of their position to micromanage everyone. They keep all the "perks" of ministry and flaunt these in front of other staff. Some rule their churches with an iron fist through guilt and heavy-handedness. Some set unrealistic quotas for attendance, home visits, and baptisms. Many of these pastors usually have short tenures, constant staff turnover, and disgruntled congregations. This is not the suggested way to encourage positive staff relationships.

Other pastors, however, try to share leadership with their associates. These pastors, while held ultimately accountable, recognize the importance of sharing perks, authority, and position. They model flexibility and servant leadership to the staff ministers and their congregations. Pastors who share with and empower their staffs are more likely to develop deeper loyalties and are more likely to grow their associates into prominent places of leadership. These pastors usually have longer staff tenures and happy congregations. They understand that kindness and respect of colleagues go a long way in helping build healthy staff relationships.

However, most pastors are less sensitive to staff relationships, shared ministries, and multiple responsibilities than are staff ministers. This "lower sensitivity" is not because they are uncaring, out of touch, or overly authoritative. Pastors, generally, are simply more concerned with the "macro" (or broader) vision and leadership needs of the church. Pastors are also not as sensitive to the inner workings of staff relationships on a day-to-day basis because of the pressures of their own position. Staff ministers must share their feelings and needs with their pastor and keep the pastor informed.

Rule #1 for relating to the pastor: If you can't say something good about someone (even the pastor), say nothing! Staff ministers need to be more sensitive to the pastor. Staff should be loyal and supportive. The pastor is the "head" of the staff. Staff ministers may disagree privately, but in public, staff ministers should be seen as partners with the pastor. Sometimes this is difficult. You may disagree in a staff meeting or in the pastor's office, but once a decision is made, staff must be supportive of the pastor. We are to put the welfare of the church and the staff ahead of our own. Whining, speaking out disagreeably, or publicly confronting the pastor will do no one in the church any good.

Staff ministers often miss opportunities to display loyalty. Disgruntled parishioners seek out those willing to agree with them. Complainers want to go to people who will sympathize. If someone comes to you with complaints, tell them of your support for the pastor and suggest they go directly to the pastor with their thoughts. People will try to "triangle" us into their arguments. Our job is to be a "less anxious" presence in their lives. Be careful that these negative members don't trap you in their web of negativity.

The responses that follow are from staff in reaction to pastoral criticism from groups within the church. These are not suggested for building unity and positive staff relationships.

- "Well, if I were the pastor, we surely would not be doing things this way!"
- "Well, sure he is not a very strong pastor or preacher, but he is a good guy!"
- "I know things are not good, but she is the pastor!"
- "She came and things have not improved, and until she leaves, she is what we have got!"

- "I think he does a good job; I just do not know what he does all day!"
- "Well, if he were in the office more, things would be running a lot smoother!"

The above statements lead to animosity and disunity among the staff and church family. These statements also reflect as negatively on the staff minister as on the pastor. The congregation loses respect for the pastor and staff in such situations.

Perhaps a more positive response would be, "I am sorry you feel that way. Have you shared your feelings with our pastor? I have always found him/her open to my needs. You should make an appointment and talk to him/her."

Rule #2 for relating to the pastor: Have a private meeting at least once a month with the senior pastor. We are all busy people! The same goes for pastor and ministry associates. There are times when ministers can go for days without seeing each other. The weekly staff meeting is filled with coordinating the calendar, sharing people needs, and communicating critical information. There is hardly time for sharing personal visions and making sure staff ministers are "in sync" with each other. The monthly private meeting allows you and the pastor time to reacquaint yourselves with each other, to share personal insights, and to laugh together.

Ask for an hour and take thirty minutes! But make sure you get personal time each month. Take the pastor to lunch or out for midday snack. Visit the hospital with the pastor, go on an outreach visit together, attend a conference. There are many opportunities to share time with the pastor without adding to already busy schedules.

You probably will not become the pastor's best friend. That is not the goal anyway. The goal is to build a professional relationship with the pastor and to build loyalty and respect. Socializing will bring about friendship, but do not expect that you are "Tonto" to the pastor's "Lone Ranger"! Expect an encouraging and professional relationship with the pastor. Pay attention to the boundaries the pastor sets and enjoy the relationship that develops.

Rule #3 for relating to the pastor: Nobody likes bad surprises! Keeping the pastor informed in all situations is an important role in our ministries. Negative surprises quickly bring conflict and confrontation. Every opportunity must be taken to inform and keep the pastor from being "blind-sided."

As we have already mentioned, the pastor is busy and involved in many of the "big picture" issues of congregation management. As staff ministers, we are managing the more specialized or "micro" issues of the congregation. Staff and pastor must be on the same page. If you anticipate conflict in your ministry, inform the pastor immediately. All significant expenditures, policy changes, people problems, or program shifts should be communicated to the pastor as quickly as possible. Inform the pastor in writing and verbally. Never think that telling the pastor something significant while you are on the way to the water cooler will suffice. Bad surprises can get you fired. Keep the pastor informed.

The pastor needs to know pertinent information ahead of time to react intelligently when a problem arises. An informed pastor gives confidence to the membership. If the pastor is informed, the congregation will also build confidence in you!

Rule #4 for relating to the pastor: If you set up a win/lose situation with your pastor, you will always lose. The potential for a power struggle with the pastor is always possible. Do not fall into this trap! The pastor is always the head of the staff. If you want to be the head of staff, go somewhere and be a pastor. Staff "power plays" never result in good endings for staff ministers, the pastor, or the church.

While most of us will rarely threaten the pastor on purpose, many of us overstep our boundaries without even realizing it. Stay intentional about your ministry. Constantly ask yourself, "If I were the pastor, how would I perceive this action?" If the action would threaten you, the odds are good that you have overstepped your area of ministry. Be careful how far you push this line. Does this mean you do not preach in the pastor's absence? Does this mean you do not lead without consulting the pastor on your every decision? Does this mean you do not run your own program? Of course not! This does mean that you think through scenarios before you act. Too many of us have acted spontaneously (and with the best of intentions) only to find that we have gone too far. Few staff ministers succeed without pastoral support. Do not threaten the pastor. Seek teamwork, keep the pastor informed, and lead with integrity. The worst thing you can do is to "think" you are making the best decision possible without having done your homework and without thinking the decision all the way through. Be a person of credibility and integrity. As you live this example, pastor and congregation will come to respect you and trust you.

Rule #5 for relating to the pastor: Every job description ends with "and other duties as assigned by the pastor." There will be days when you've finished your work and are headed home to relax, but suddenly the pastor calls. There is an emergency that needs to be covered, and you are the only one the pastor could reach. This is one of those times you might be tempted to say, "No! That's not my job!" Resist the impulse and tend to the emergency with grace and professionalism. You want to be seen as a credible and versatile minister.[3] Listen, follow through, be flexible, and respond with positive energy. Credibility means building trusting relationships. Covering emergencies means you can be trusted, even if this is not in your ministry area or your job description. You are in control of your own professionalism. Act in a professional manner even when you are frustrated. Be a professional in every aspect of your ministry, even if it is not in your job description.

TEAM—Together Everyone Accomplishes More

Good teams function together as one unit. The best staff teams cover for one another, share the joys, and support each other in frustrations. My introductory statement to church staffs with which I have been privileged to serve is "I promise to be your best cheerleader!"

The meanings behind the statement are important.

• Cheerleaders don't compete with the team; they support the team and enlist other support.
• Cheerleaders don't take away from the action on the field; they rally the fans to energize the team.
• Cheerleaders find ways to do their own thing while supporting the total work of the team.
• Cheerleaders encourage others to get involved with the team and take interest in the game.
• Cheerleaders are professionals in their own right; yet, they know they are only as successful as the team.
• Cheerleaders do not threaten the team's performance, criticize the leaders of the team, or hog the spotlight.

Being a cheerleader is important to my ministry. We will only be as successful in our individual ministries as the team is successful in our combined ministries. Loyalty to one another is crucial. Public conflict between staff is crippling. Communication among team members is critical.

Staff members are accountable for their own performance, resource management, and time on the job. However, the team members can support the staff minister who might be struggling. Team members can assist in programming. Too often we either ignore the staff minister who is struggling or we are thankful that the pressure is on someone else. The team works together for the advancement of the total work of the church, for the total advancement of the kingdom of God!

Lyle Schaller in *The Multiple Staff and the Larger Church* outlines the "7 C's of Staff Relationships": compatibility, continuity, competence, confidence, coherence, complementary relationships, and conceptualization of the role in regards to the particular congregation.[4] A closer look at each of these may provide a positive model of the characteristics for productive staff relationships.

(1) *Compatibility.* Compatibility speaks to how well the staff ministers work and play together. This trait speaks to the passion, harmony, and unity of the staff.

This trait assumes no superstars among the staff. There are staff members—namely the pastor and music minister—who have "face time" every week. Visibility in the worship services of the church creates an assumed importance before the congregation. Compatible staffs seek to give equality of visibility. The sensitive pastor or music minister (the planner of worship) seeks to provide opportunities for all staff members to lead in worship. Find ways to involve all staff ministers in using their worship gifts to lead the congregation.

Find ways to involve all staff ministers in other programs of the church as well. During Vacation Bible School, all staff ministers should be present and interacting with the children. During youth camp, all staff ministers should be present and building relationships with the youth. Ministers should be involved in every aspect of congregational life—teaching, preaching, praying, building fellowship, and leading in worship. That is not to say that all staff members are involved heavily in every ministry of the church. This is to suggest that when big events are happening, we are sensitive to include each staff minister in the event. The compatible staff finds ways to play together. Going out to lunch once a week is a team-building activity. Going to an amusement park, to a pool, or to the movies together helps build fellowship among the staff ministers. When playing together, the staff loosens inhibitions and is more real. As you play, you let down your "professional stiffness" and share more of your true selves. Be intentional about finding ways to play together.

The compatible staff also shares in ministry events together. Doing hospital visitations and outreach visits allow times of sharing and team-building. Sharing in ministry tasks, praying together, and even leading committee meetings together also provide times for informal sharing and fellowship. The sensitive leader/pastor will find times for one-on-one sharing with staff ministers and will also engage in total staff sharing. Staff retreats that allow for time away together also help build relationships. These retreats combine planning, visioning, sharing, and playing.

(2) *Continuity.* The staff that stays together grows closer and more comfortable with one another. The average length of service for ministers is now less than four years.[5] Longevity of service allows the minister to understand the inner workings of the congregation. Longevity allows the minister time to build relationships and put in place procedures for getting things done. This is found in a recent newsletter for *The Church Leadership Network*: "The optimum good long-term tenure is somewhere between seven and fifteen years. Several congregational studies point out that the most productive year for clergy is actually the seventh! It is usually after the seventh year that substantial growth takes place."[6]

As we share tenure together, we begin to anticipate one another. We know when colleagues are struggling, when they are stressed, and when they are happy. As we share tenure together, we are better able to trust each other. As we grow in our trust for one another, we are better able to grow in our unity of service to the congregation.

The church is becoming what the church staff already is! The congregation follows the lead of its leaders. A staff that is unified, excited, and energetic will form a congregation that is unified, excited, and energetic about doing church. A healthy staff leads to a healthy congregation. As we lead with continuity, we develop better members. As we develop better members, they encourage us to become even better leaders. This cycle builds stronger, more positive congregations. We all encourage each other. Now *that* is church!

(3) *Competence.* Obviously, hiring competent and professional staff is crucial. Ministers must operate with a high degree of professionalism. Congregations have high expectations of their staff ministers. They pay us good money to do good work. Our work is a reflection of the congregation. Many in the congregation are professional people. Many work in high-stress situations.

They are driven by excellence and quality every day. They expect the same high degree of professionalism from their spiritual leaders.

Effective leaders are never content to be average. Most ministers have educated themselves beyond the basic college degree. Most ministers have gotten training from credible sources to lead congregations. Let your leadership reflect the competence with which you have been trained. Continue to grow and build on your experience. Obviously, you cannot bring twenty years of experience to your first ministry position. Seek out every training opportunity (that time and money will allow) to continue your education and professionalism.

Leaders lead others. Competent leaders do not try to do everything. Competent leaders lead others to insure that everything gets done. Competent leaders do not try to meet every need. Competent leaders lead others to see that all needs are met. Competent leaders do not try to be all things to all people. Competent leaders develop partners who will help broaden the scope of the church's ministry. Competent leaders build trust, teamwork, and unity!

(4) *Confidence.* Professional behavior elicits trust and confidence from the congregation. As you work hard and work smart, the confidence in your leadership grows. Doing the right things and doing things right exhibits professionalism and builds confidence. Working with confidence also instills confidence in those with whom you work. Confidence breeds confidence.

Preach, teach, and lead worship with quality. There will be events that tug at you. There will be emergencies that pop up and pull at your time and energy. Still, never make excuses for a poor performance. Nothing will kill the confidence of your congregation or your colleagues like whining, procrastination, and poor performance.

Sunday morning is your main priority. Make sure you set aside time each week to allow you to be confident in your Sunday morning responsibilities. Whether you lead worship, teach Bible study, or simply greet people at the door, be confident in your professionalism.

When people and organizational needs have taken up too much of your time and preparation, you still will have to deliver with confidence. Your congregation and colleagues know when you have had a hard week and have been pushed to the limit. Present like a pro. You will instill confidence in your colleagues and your congregation. Never let them see you sweat!

(5) *Coherence.* Staff ministers spend a tremendous amount of time making sure all the ministries of the church flow together. Staff ministers have to share in a team approach to ministry. All the ministries must flow toward the same goal. Committees must also make sure they are working toward the same goals. The staff guides and directs the work of the church to make sure everyone is moving toward the same goals.

The starting point for coherence is a church mission and vision statement. The mission/vision statement provides a direction for the church for about eighteen months to two years. This should be formulated in an annual staff-planning meeting. After the staff agrees on direction, the mission/vision is then presented to deacons, committee chairs, and other program leaders for their support. After these have agreed, the statement is then presented to the church for agreement.

Upon the completion of a mission/vision statement, the whole congregation knows the main direction of the work of the church. All programming is then evaluated on whether or not the activities are supporting the mission/vision direction. The mission/vision sets the tone.

The staff meeting "fine-tunes" the direction. Staff meetings should be conducted with consistency each week. This is a time of praying, communicating, evaluating, and redirecting. All staff should be "equal" when they come to this meeting. While the pastor sets the tone, each minister should have the freedom to agree or disagree, to question, and to ask for clarification. This interchange should happen with openness and collegiality. The staff meeting keeps each of us accountable to one another and keeps the entire staff accountable to the mission/vision statement.

As we keep ourselves focused on a unifying statement and direction of ministry, we are able to plan and minister with intentionality. Programming with intentionality lets us agree on direction and priorities. Intentionality allows us to share resources and be respectful of the time and availability of our members. Programming with intentionality also allows us to be supportive of each of the other staff ministers. When we are all pulling in the same direction, we are able to support one another. Intentionality means that we work with direction and unity. Intentionality keeps us working as a team and growing together![7]

(6) *Complementary Relationships.* This area describes how we fit together as a staff. We each bring gifts and abilities to our ministry. If all staff ministers have the same strengths, we are not complementary; we are one-dimensional. Churches should call staff ministers who complement one another.

Some churches call ministers to conform with one another and to the personality of the church. Some churches call ministers and throw them into competition with one another. Some churches call ministers who spend an enormous amount of time in conflict with the other staff and the congregation. The most effective churches call ministers who compliment one another.

Complementary relationships speak to balance! A balance of ministry skills and personalities means the staff will better support one another. One minister may have strength in evangelism, while another has strength for hospital visitation. One minister may be stronger at counseling, while another is strong in activities. Too many churches call ministers who all have the same strengths. That means "holes" will exist in the overall ministry of the church. We should call ministers to work to one another's strengths. Many churches, however, prefer to call a group of "ministerial clones" who all exhibit the same set of skills.

A balanced staff will be happier and enjoy working together. They will not be threatened by one another and will not compete with each other. Complementary relationships lead to healthy church staffs.

(7) *Conceptualization.* This speaks to a congruence of ministry to the individual congregation. Too often, ministers come to a church, put in play a set of ministry programs, and when they run out of programs, they simply go to the next church and work through their "bag of tricks" again. This approach to ministry does not show much congruence to a particular congregation, nor does it show professional growth. While all ministers have a basic skill set of programs and approaches, these must be tailored to reflect an understanding of the particular church setting in which the minister serves.

The mission/vision statement will help keep ministers focused on the needs of the church in which they serve. The weekly staff meeting will also help. Pastoral leadership will help set the direction and help staff ministers acclimate to the particular church setting. The temptation is to do the same program we presented in the previous place (or places) of service. However, this approach to ministry stifles growth in the minister and robs the church of creative leadership. We must make every effort through our own personal growth, training, planning, and prayer to stay fresh!

Servant-leadership

Servant-leadership is a philosophy developed by Robert Greenleaf in the late 1960s. Greenleaf described servant-leadership in his groundbreaking book, *The Servant as Leader,* in 1970: "The servant-leader is servant first.

Conscious choice brings one then to aspire to lead. The servant-first leader takes care to make sure that other people's highest priority needs are being served."[8]

Many a minister has had "servanthood" drilled into his/her brain during ministry training. However, the model of servant taught to many was that of "suffering servant" or even "suffering slave." That is not the model Greenleaf proposed. Servant-first leadership puts people first in order to help them grow and develop. Servant-leadership attempts to help enhance "the personal growth of workers and improve the quality and caring of our many institutions through a combination of teamwork, community building, personal involvement in decision making, and ethical and caring behavior."[9]

Servant-leadership is built upon a covenant relationship between leadership and follower-ship. The servant-leader takes time to listen, shares empathy, seeks to be an instrument of healing, is a good steward of time and resources, and is committed to helping others grow personally and in the context of community. Servant-leadership communicates a caring and intentional relationship with the congregation.

Servant-leadership does away with typical authoritative and hierarchical organization. Servant-leadership stresses collaboration, teamwork, and mutual respect between ministerial colleagues and in the congregation. This philosophy requires a high degree of professional respect for the gifts and abilities of staff colleagues. Further, this calls for empowerment, trust, shared leadership, and sharing. The "Lone Ranger" minister doing all things for all people or the "Godfather" pastor giving orders and bossing others will not survive long in today's "postmodern" church.[10]

Servant-leadership is developed through abandoning our judgmental attitudes. The servant-leader listens and evaluates objectively, shares power and authority, and continues to develop leaders. Servant-leadership encourages all to put away their egos and share equally in the duties of the team. The servant-leader embraces people, developing them and caring for them. The servant-leader is committed to growing everyone in the organization!

The key to growing and developing servant-leadership is sacrifice. The benefits for a staff of servant-leaders will lead to a growing and sharing staff of ministers. Positive staff relationships are difficult to build and maintain. This is not because we don't care about one another. Mainly, we get too busy and begin taking our staff relationships for granted. Staff relationships will only grow as we spend time sharing, growing, praying, and ministering together.

Successful church staffs have an agreed-upon mission; have an unselfishness of work and ministry tasks; have a high level of professional competence and long tenures; take care of themselves while taking care of others; and have a high degree of trust and loyalty.

Share openly with one another. Build trust. Trust God. Live on bravely, working hard and sharing together. As you do, you will grow in a deep appreciation of your staff colleagues, and they will grow in their appreciation of you. Your church will grow in these areas, too!

• **Bo Prosser** *is Coordinator for Congregational Life with the Cooperative Baptist Fellowship and has served many years in the local church.*

NOTES

[1] Bo Prosser, Charles Qualls, *Lessons from the Cloth* (Macon: Smyth & Helwys, 1999).

[2] George Barna, "Pastors Paid Better, Attendance Unchanged" <www.barna.org> (29 March 2001).

[3] "Senior Pastors, On What It's Like Working With You," *Youthworker Journal* <www.youthspecialties.com> (fall 1995).

[4] Lyle Schaller, *The Multiple Staff and the Larger Church* (Nashville: Abingdon Press, 1980).

[5] George Barna, "Research Trends" <www.barna.org> (2001).

[6] "Church Champions Update for August 6, 2001," *Leadership Network* <LNextra@leadnet.org> (2001).

[7] For more on mission/vision and coherence in leadership, consult B. Nanus, *Visionary Leadership* (San Francisco: Jossey-Bass, 1992); L. Bolman and T. Deal, *Reframing Organizations*, 2d ed. (San Francisco: Jossey-Bass, 1997).

[8] Robert Greenleaf, *The Servant as Leader* (Indianapolis, 1970); excerpt taken from the Greenleaf Center for Servant-Leadership web page <www.greenleaf.org>.

[9] Ibid., as quoted by Larry Spears, CEO of the Greenleaf Center.

[10] For discussions on post-modernism and shared leadership, see Leonard Sweet, *Aquachurch* (Loveland, CO: Group Publishing, 1999); also see <www.leonardsweet.com>.

Bo Prosser

Working with Volunteers and Caring for People

"People go where they know they have been prepared for and are cared for!"[1]

This has been my mission statement for many years. Regardless of your position on a church staff, you are in the "people business"! Enlisting, developing, and caring for volunteer leaders is one of the most critical challenges for church leaders today. Sharing leadership responsibilities and authority with volunteers through a "servant leadership" approach is equally challenging. Preparing for and caring for people must be a priority of your ministry activities.

A colleague of mine remarked recently, "Church work would be a wonderful vocation if it were not for church members!" Another colleague has said often, "It is not that I have to go to every committee meeting. But they do such crazy things when I am not there!" Obviously, neither of these two ministers put their focus on the "people business."

However, if we are going to be successful in our ministry, we will only do so through the relationships we establish with our congregations. People are always available to serve and participate, but they may not always be motivated to do so. Guilt will only motivate for a short while. Obligation may last a bit longer. Empowered and challenged volunteers will serve with joy for long stretches of time. As we utilize the skills and energies of people and as we care for the people in our congregations, our churches will thrive and our ministries will be more fulfilling than we ever imagined.

Who Are "Volunteers" and What Can They Do?

Volunteers have a variety of desires and motivations. Most people in our churches want to feel useful and want to make a difference in their faith and church. They may lead a children's choir, teach a Sunday school class, hand out bulletins, or clean the sanctuary after worship. For the most part, volunteers are well-meaning, good-hearted, and Christ-loving folk. They are invaluable to the work of the church.

In several churches where I have served, a group of members have met for Bible study and service each week. We would conduct a short devotion and prayer time and then turn the volunteers loose for all sorts of service. They delivered flowers to shut-ins, visited nursing homes, duplicated tapes of worship and delivered them, helped in the church office, helped in the church kitchen, washed windows, filed documents, folded bulletins, etc. Get the picture?

Volunteers come with competence and are willing to work hard and pitch in. Some of them possess skills that are directly related to the work of the church. Some have skills that don't relate to the church. Still, they always come willing to serve.

One of my favorite volunteers became a friend and mentor. He had been a career missionary. When he retired, he wanted to "help out" around the church. He came humbly every week and washed windows, trimmed hedges, or did anything else we asked. For several weeks, he helped organize my library. I was embarrassed to ask for his help, but he was eager to share. He became a special friend and valued mentor. He helped me understand that people matter. He demonstrated the importance of relationships with parishioners.

People are looking for something that makes a difference.[2] They come to us looking for ways to involve themselves in meaningful service. Part of our ministry is to help them find meaningful places to serve. Part of our ministry is to find ways to motivate others in our congregations for meaningful service. Ministry opportunities abound! Our task is to match the right people with the right opportunities. When called to meaningful ministry, they will respond willingly and competently. Any organization dependent upon volunteer energy soon recognizes that it cannot function without a core of volunteers.

What Do Volunteers Need?

Volunteers in the church want to add depth and meaning to their spiritual lives and share their faith with others. Many find that the best way for them to witness is not with evangelistic pleas but through meaningful service. Think about this: volunteers staff all the committees, service ministries, teaching ministries, and most of the financial and administrative functions of the church. Volunteers are active ministers in the lives of our churches.

While vital to the life of a congregation, volunteers are a challenging lot. They sometimes cause frustration. Occasionally, they cause problems (or at least opportunities for improvement). Volunteers are human beings with their own set of feelings, understandings, and biases. Sometimes their emotions get in the way. Sometimes their understandings are not as complete as those of their leaders. Sometimes they think they know more or better than leadership. Regardless of the shortcomings that arise, however, we cannot do effective ministry without them.

What do volunteers need to keep them functioning at high levels of positive, forward-thinking energy?

Suggestions for Healthy, Happy Volunteers

The suggestions offered below are not intended as the final word in dealing with the nurturing of volunteers. Current literature is filled with lists and suggestions for how to keep a happy workforce. There are many resources for dealing with leadership and motivating volunteers. The following thoughts are simply a way to begin discussion.

(1) *Pray, pray, pray.* First and foremost, bathe each of these suggestions in prayer! A disciplined prayer life is central to effective leadership. It is the foundation upon which all the following suggestions are built. Staying in close communication with God keeps you grounded and spiritually strong. The first task of volunteer work is enlisting the right people. Praying with discipline leads you to the people needed to get the job done.

Leadership is never easy. These suggestions will make your job easier. Even without prayer, you may succeed occasionally. However, a disciplined prayer life will give you the spiritual power you need to make sound decisions, to stay focused, and to be an effective leader.

(2) *Community is crucial.* Take time to build relationships. The people you lead must understand your vision and priorities. They must understand that you are a person of integrity and consistency. Loren Mead of the Alban Institute shares, "A key leadership issue has been how the ordained leader understood and acted out her or his role in relationship to how the lay leaders understood and practiced their roles."[3]

While your presence will reveal something of your character and philosophy, nothing can take the place of one-on-one relationships. Make small group sharing a priority on your calendar. Such groups are slow to develop and require your dedicated time; however, the intimacy of small group relationships will help your ministry. Jesus made relationships part of his foundation for ministry. So should we!

Who are the key leaders in your ministry? Which leaders need to be clued in to your vision and mission? Identify key leaders in your circle of influence and begin building relationships with them.

Set aside one day a week for breakfast or lunch with someone you want to get to know better. Set aside one day a week to meet with the key leader of your ministry. Set aside one hour a day for phoning volunteers who are instrumental in leadership of your ministry areas.

In almost every church I have served, Thursday lunch has been my meeting time for working and sharing with my key leaders. This hour is blocked out on my calendar and it rarely gets interrupted. During these times of fellowship and sharing, we get to know one another. We share hopes and dreams, not only for our ministry, but also for our lives. We get to know one another and to love and appreciate one another.

My phone calling usually takes place on a Saturday afternoon. I call folks who need a bit of encouragement or a pat on the back. My script is simple: "Hi, I am calling to say I am thinking of you. I appreciate who you are and what you do for our church! Is everything okay with you?" Then I pause and allow them to tell me whatever is on their mind. Generally, this kind of call takes about two minutes and ten or more leaders can be touched in a short time.

Phone calls may seem superficial and impersonal, but your heartfelt and genuine concern can make a great impact. Try it for a month and you will begin to see a difference in your ministry and in the leadership of your volunteers.

These calls are not to "talk business." They are not to make anyone feel guilty. They are not gossip. The purpose of each call is simply to say, "Thank you for what you do!" We are inundated with calls soliciting money, selling items, and trying to manipulate us. A thank-you phone call from a familiar voice is appreciated and unforgettable.

Spend significant energy building relationships. The more you do to involve yourself in the lives of your leaders, the more they will do to involve themselves in your ministry. The more we work together in mutual support, the more effective (and less conflicting) our ministry becomes!

(3) *Trust volunteers to do their work.* Trust takes time. Trust is built on relationships and respect. Remember that you have enlisted, trained, and entrusted highly motivated and highly competent people with important tasks. Let them do their jobs!

There is nothing more frustrating than being micromanaged. None of us likes to have someone looking over our shoulders, second-guessing our every move or decision. When you assign tasks, allow volunteers to do their jobs. Current management literature calls this "empowerment."

"Empowerment" is letting people do what we have asked them to do. Not practicing empowerment is often the downfall of leaders. Most adults do not need to be micromanaged or overly controlled. We have to empower our volunteers to make decisions. We have to trust them to lead within their frame of responsibility. As we empower others, they learn that we can trust them. Empowerment builds trust and leads to competence both in the leader and the volunteer. When volunteers know we trust them, they are more motivated to work with and for us.

Peter Drucker speaks to this issue: "Organizations are based on trust. Trust means that you know what to expect of people. Trust means mutual understanding."[4]

The administrative staff in a church I served had continually asked for my input in day-to-day decisions that they should have been handling. After two or three days of this, we had a staff meeting. I shared a poster with each assistant that displayed the following words: "In every situation, I trust you to make the best decision!" After the meeting, the staff still brought decisions to me. I gently reminded them of my trust. Then I asked, "What do you suggest?" Their suggestions were always appropriate. My response was, "Go do it!"

After two or three days, they stopped bringing routine questions to my office. Though I told them I trusted them, they needed me to prove myself to them. The office ran smoothly after that experience.

(4) *Listen actively.* Listening takes practice. We all listen, or at least we hear! But to truly listen we have to pay attention to what is said. We hear with our ears, but we listen with our eyes *and* our ears.

As people come to you to talk, remove distractions on your desk, turn your phone to "do not disturb," and look at the person who is talking to you. Give the person your eyes and your brain. As you pay attention to people, they will know you care about them. When they know that you care about them, they will know they can trust you as a leader.

Active listening takes practice and patience. Especially in today's world of multitasking and sensory bombardment, most of us have to work at being an attentive, active listener. Many management gurus tell us of the primary importance of active listening. Current management literature devotes significant space to the practice of developing this important skill.

I once worked with a pastor who never paid attention to me in private meetings. I had to talk to him between phone calls, interruptions from his secretary, and his own inattentiveness. Meeting with him was frustrating! If he did talk with me and no one interrupted, as soon as something I said sparked a thought in him, he reached across his desk and jotted a note to himself. Talking to him was a distraction; I finally quit trying. I would send him memos or talk to him on the phone! Needless to say, I neither felt prepared for nor cared for in my relationship with him.

Active listening communicates to the other person that he or she matters to you and has something significant to share. This is especially important in working with volunteers. Active listening serves us well as we work as manager, minister, and motivator.

(5) *Be intentional.* Intentionality is one of the most difficult disciplines to develop. Intentionality keeps us focused on the main things. So many things clamor for our attention every day; we must be intentional about staying on course and following through. Being intentional means that "come heaven or high water," I will do what I have set my mind to do.

Distractions are everywhere. Even as you read these words, there are distractions all around you. Being intentional means that you not only read these words, but you also pay attention to what you read. Intentionality means you pay attention and stay focused on doing what you said you will do.

One way to stay intentional is to devise a mission/vision statement and stay focused on that statement. This statement should be a sentence that describes who you are and what your purpose is. The sentence should be fifteen words or less—the shorter the better. "People go, where they know, they have been prepared for and are cared for!" has been my guiding statement for years. This sentence helps me stay intentional about preparing for and caring for those with whom I minister. Whether my ministry audience is a Sunday morning congregation, a Bible study group, a choir, or even a reader of my writing, my mission/vision statement keeps me intentional. Take a moment and write your own mission/vision. Keep practicing and focus on your philosophy of ministry. Then write it out and stay focused on what you decide.

(6) *Affirm and celebrate constantly.* There are several things that keep me motivated in working with volunteers. We celebrate little victories. We try to

make 100 things 1 percent better. We try to catch people doing good things. We try to acknowledge people who do good things well.

The volunteer force is competent and motivated, but everybody needs affirmation. Affirmation again communicates that you care and that you have noticed. Affirmation lets people know they are important to the organization and to you. You cannot affirm people enough.

Here are ways to affirm your volunteers:

- Send birthday cards.
- Send words of affirmation and thanks via e-mail and fax.
- Send personal handwritten notes of thanks.
- Offer public affirmation from the pulpit.
- Send flowers for special occasions.
- Send greeting cards for special occasions or to say thanks.
- Express thanks through church bulletins and newsletters.
- Express thanks through a church "Brag Board" or bulletin board.
- Send "free meal" tickets good for a Wednesday night supper.
- Set aside a "Special People" table for Wednesday nights.
- Make phone calls simply to say thank you.

The above are only a few ways to affirm others. There are thousands of ways to say thank you. The important part is that you say thanks! Affirm people when they do good things. Affirm people even when they may not meet your expectations. Affirm that they have a ministry and that what they are doing is important to God.

While you affirm your people for their ministries, remember to celebrate significant congregational achievements. Too often we are so busy maintaining the program and trying to pull off one more event that we forget to celebrate. God is doing great things every day.

Celebrations don't have to be elaborate parties. They can be affirmations taken to a congregational level. Take time to celebrate! Volunteers need to be noticed and affirmed. Celebrations need to occur to build community, provide affirmation, and keep everyone motivated and functioning at high levels.

Here are examples of celebrations:

- Banquets for workers at the end of a year
- Public recognition of your teaching faculty
- Fellowships for saying thank you

• Commissioning services for mission work or for teachers and leaders
• Prayer gatherings to celebrate God's blessings

There are thousands of ways to celebrate. The important thing is that you are not too busy that you fail to notice and celebrate the goodness of God in the life of your ministries.

(7) *Equip for more effective ministry.* You may have the best group of volunteers in the world, but if you do not equip them, do not expect them to do good work. Equipping your volunteers with the tools they need is crucial for making good things happen. Volunteers need periodic training events to keep them functioning at effective levels. Too often we enlist someone for a particular job, shake their hand to welcome them, hand them their teaching materials, and send them off without another word. Instead, we must stay in constant contact with volunteers.

Just as we have to affirm volunteers, build community, and stay in contact with them, we also have to equip them.

Here are a few approaches to equipping:

• Conduct an annual weekend training event.
• Conduct quarterly evening training events.
• Establish mentors to aid in the learning curve.
• Establish online, computer-based training events.
• Customize e-mails and faxes in a "newsletter" format.
• Purchase special equipment or tools for quality training.
• Make sure literature is ordered and delivered early.
• Communicate special events and special needs.
• Help volunteers help each other.
• Help volunteers help themselves.
• Share phone numbers of helpers.
• Conduct annual committee orientation gatherings.

Keep finding ways to make sure your volunteers have everything they need to do quality ministry.

Training includes a transfer of previous experience and the addition of new information. Training also includes understanding the "big picture" of how the church works, your philosophy of ministry and your mission/vision, and how ministry functions within the total life of the church. Volunteers need to be trained in the area of financial resources, budgeting procedures, policy and constitutional issues, people resources, and procedural issues for doing the work. Train them, equip them, and turn them loose to do the work.

Training is not static. As the needs of the church change, so will the needs of those who come for training. Training needs will vary. Some people will have served previously; others will be novices. Try to meet the needs of the people in a way that equips them for the most effective levels of ministry. Try to find ways to customize the training that will make the most effective and efficient use of your time and their time. Break training into small bites. Let people choose the levels of depth they feel they need.

Time pressures, budget pressures, and ministry demands will always press us in our training approaches. Usually, the first thing to go when pressures mount is training. Do not give in to the pressures that will try to pull you from continuing training measures. The more you equip volunteers, the better they minister.

(8) *Give volunteers flexibility.* While this is a close cousin to empowerment, flexibility is more than simply empowering volunteers to work. When we empower them, we move out of the way and give them the freedom they need to do the work. We also model flexibility for them; there is more than just *my* way to do ministry.

We are in the midst of huge cultural shifts. Denominational loyalty is at an all-time low. Younger generations are rebelling against institutionalism, even that of the church. Leadership integrity and credibility have been rocked by recent scandals from the presidency to the pulpit. These "cultural earthquakes" have radically changed the way of doing church as we have known it. Changes have caused shifts in behaviors we exhibit, in our workplace boundaries, and in the fragile balance of power within the institution. Change can cause conflict and insecurity. Change makes us uneasy.

In the face of cultural earthquakes, we have to allow for flexibility of leadership from our volunteers. We have to let them know there are many ways of accomplishing the same goal. As we equip and empower our volunteers, we also give them flexibility to do their jobs. If we choke their flexibility, we stifle their creativity and motivation. Christian service marches to the leadership of a radical Christ. The Holy Spirit takes our creative abilities and enhances our insights and ideas. The effective leader allows volunteers to use their own relationships with the Holy Spirit to find viable solutions.

Bob Dale, in his book *Leading Edge*, shares several suggestions for stretching our imaginations and keeping us flexible as we do God's work.[5]

- Read widely, and include out-of-the-ordinary titles or topics.
- Travel to places you have never visited.
- Listen more than you talk.
- Break an old routine.
- Discuss life with someone whom you know holds a different point of view.
- Become an expert on something.
- Take different routes to routine destinations.
- Ask "what if" questions.
- Play, laugh, and keep a sense of humor.

In addition, I would like to add a couple more.

- Play worst-case scenario. Ask yourself what is the worst that can happen.
- Find ways to develop your creativity. Look at the world in creative ways.
- Ride a carousel.
- Sing, play an instrument, write a poem, or act.
- Learn from your mistakes.
- Be aware of your blessings.

The key to flexibility is to seek balance. We must continually ask the question, "Is this best for the largest group of people in the church, or is this a part of my own agenda?" The call to community (to be God's people) must come before personal agendas, small group preferences, or even power people.

(9) *Focus more on ministry and less on programs.* There is always a tendency to maintain the status quo and slip into complacency. With time pressures on volunteers and budget constraints on resources, innovative approaches sometimes suffer or are ignored altogether. You will be tempted to keep doing the same old thing the same old way. George Barna, noted church researcher, challenges us to evaluate programs periodically and objectively. "The unwillingness to subject ministry programs to fair and constructive evaluations means that the church is susceptible to deterioration due to negligence."[6] Keep the faith, keep your focus, love people, and minister to them. Milliken and Company, a world leader in textiles, has a definition for "insanity" that I think probably originated from a Baptist church. According to a sign in their corporate offices, "Insanity is doing what you have always done in the past and expecting different results!"[7]

Stay fresh in your prayer life and in your spiritual growth. Focus on people. Do the right things and do things right. Care for your people, pray for them, love them, affirm them, and grow with them.

Caring for People

The way you pay attention to the volunteers in your congregation reflects the way you care for people in your church. More than simply meeting needs, ministry is teaching people to "be one another" with one another.[8] Peter Steinke says that congregations are unique and complex institutions. According to Steinke, all congregations are working with a small set of core issues:[9]

• Mission and how to achieve it
• Strengths and resources and how to implement them
• Anxiety and how to manage it
• Wholeness and how to maintain it

In order to meet the needs and respond to the core issues as defined by Steinke and others, we must continually care for our members. Caring for them includes equipping and empowering them to care for one another. Steinke has employed the word *metanoia* as a means for managing these core values and growing toward wholeness: "People who repent, who are in their right minds, take responsibility for what they have done . . . they seek forgiveness for themselves. And likewise, they forgive. Grace commits to the future, to a new creation. Metanoia is the antidote for paranoia . . . to forgive is to release."[10]

As we care for people, we follow through on making the church a better place for today and the days to come. We are the handiwork of our God. We are also God's instruments. We are here to love one another and to be one another with each other!

The bottom line of caring for people, indeed caring for volunteers, comes from Christ. My paraphrase of Matthew 22:37-39 has become the baseline for everything I do in ministry: "Love the Lord God with your whole being, your heart, soul, mind, and lifestyle. And love the people on your pathway as much as you love yourself!"

• *Bo Prosser* is Coordinator for Congregational Life with the Cooperative Baptist Fellowship and has served many years in the local church.

NOTES

[1] Bo Prosser and Charles Qualls, *Lessons from the Cloth* (Macon: Smyth and Helwys, 1999).

[2] Eddie Hammett, *The Gathered and Scattered Church* (Macon: Smyth & Helwys, 1999), 33.

[3] Loren Mead, *More than Numbers: The Way Churches Grow* (Washington, DC: Alban Institute, 1993), 81.

[4] Peter Drucker, *Managing the Nonprofit Organization* (New York: Harper Collins, 1990), 116.

[5] Robert Dale, *Leading Edge: Leadership Strategies from the New Testament* (Nashville: Abingdon Press, 1996), 72-73.

[6] George Barna, *User Friendly Churches* (Venture, CA: Regal Books, 1991), 79.

[7] The Corporate Offices of Milliken and Company are located in Spartanburg, South Carolina.

[8] This idea was introduced to me at a seminar with the Center for Parish Development, 5407 South University Ave., Chicago IL, 60615; <www.missionalchurch.org>.

[9] Peter Steinke, *Healthy Congregations: A Systems Approach* (Washington, DC: Alban Institute, 1993), 41.

[10] Ibid., 88.

Mary Charlotte Ball

What an Accompanist Needs from a Music Minister

Accompanists could share the outraged cry of Rodney Dangerfield: "I get no respect!" The purpose of this chapter is to state positively the desirable qualities and attitudes that an accompanist would seek in a minister of music. Allow the following list of "R's" to be considered as essential for a good accompanist and music minister relationship.

Respect

This is mentioned first because it has been observed that many talented, caring, giving, and overlooked accompanists are not regarded as equals in the ministry of music. The music minister should regard the accompanist as a coworker. If the keyboardist is consulted, conferred with, and treated as an equal, the music program of the church will benefit from this collaboration and the effort will show in better rehearsals, services, and music ministry.

When the accompanist is treated merely as a paid musician (one who is told what to do without any explanation of purpose or total program), he or she is not part of the planning/execution process. Hiring someone to play denotes a different attitude from an approach of actually sharing with a fellow musician the plans and purpose of a music program. The author has accompanied many directors and conductors. The most enjoyable and fruitful experiences were those that were a team effort. To paraphrase the Scripture: "All things (and people) work (create music) together for good."

The accompanist needs the respect of the music minister in rearranging accompaniments for the keyboard. Many accompaniments are pianistic. Rather than entirely avoiding the organ, using the organ and piano can often orchestrate the written page more effectively. Usually the accompanist will have better knowledge of how to make this arrangement. Consultation prior to final arrangement is desirable. The music minister may desire certain elements of the accompaniment to be prominent. Any accompaniment that is merely played note for note by both keyboards fails to utilize the strengths of the organ and piano.

All of us want to be accepted and to be a part of a worthy work and ministry. If there is a lack of mutual respect between the accompanist and the minister of music, the music program may not develop as fully as desired by the church.

Rehearsal Rights

This is not an attitude or quality, but there is great importance to this "R" for the accompanist. It is necessary for the accompanist to have the rehearsal music well ahead of the scheduled rehearsal time in order to play a supportive, accurate, and efficient rehearsal. Practicing the parts and the accompaniment and getting a general overview of the text is compulsory for an effective choir rehearsal. The minister of music who gives the accompanist several new choral pieces minutes before a rehearsal promotes ulcers and headaches as well as an inefficient rehearsal. The music obviously has been selected, ordered, and received prior to the needed time. It is the right of the accompanist to have the music beforehand and to have it practiced before rehearsal.

Much of the music published today has printing errors in accidentals, voice parts, and a plethora of *da capo*s and *fines*. All of these unexpected difficulties are pitfalls for the minister of music, the accompanist, and the choir as they endeavor to read a new music selection. The choir has the right to expect their leaders to know the score and to present it correctly. The responsibility for this right lies with the music minister.

Wilson and Lyall have written of the importance of proper rehearsal preparation for the music minister: "Don't forget that the choir often follows the accompanist more than it follows conducting. Therefore, it will save time and effort if you go through the music with the accompanist in advance of the rehearsal as to tempo, dynamics and interpretation."[1]

The music minister is also expected to provide an accurate order of rehearsal numbers for the accompanist. The rehearsal cannot proceed quickly if the accompanist must look for the next announced selection. Since the ideal folder for the accompanist is a notebook with the choral numbers punched, it is imperative that the music minister inform the accompanist of the rehearsal order. A punched and cut copy reserved for the accompanist will facilitate preparation. The accompanist does not need loose pages or stubborn bindings to fight.

Most choir rehearsals use piano accompaniment. The percussiveness of the instrument enables singers to hear pitches and harmonies more easily. However, if the choral selection is to be accompanied by the organ, a rehearsal with the instrument is imperative. Proper balance between choir and organ can only be achieved when the rehearsal is in the sanctuary.

The movement of the choir from the rehearsal room into the place of worship takes rehearsal time. It also requires time for the accompanist to get to the organ, change to organ shoes, turn on the organ, adjust music, set registration, etc. The pianist does not require as much time to be ready to accompany. The music minister should be aware of these constraints and be sensitive to the organist's requirements.

One additional need that the accompanist has from the minister of music is a negative. This need applies to rehearsal as well as the Sunday service. The minister of music needs to refrain from over-conducting introductions, interludes, and the ending accompaniment (after the choir has finished singing). Obviously, the director must begin conducting the composition when eye contact has been made with the accompanist. However, continued, exaggerated motions directed to the keyboardist are unnecessary and distracting. When a soloist plays a concerto with a symphony, the symphony conductor does not direct the soloist when the orchestra ceases to play. Rather, the conductor gives a cut off to the orchestra, permits the soloist to "make music," and then directs the players in at the appropriate time. The music minister should have the same respect and confidence in the accompanist.

There is another area where sensitivity to rehearsal time is tied to respect. It is the demand that the music minister makes on the accompanist regarding soloists, ensembles, and instrumentalists scheduled for worship participation.

The music minister will expect the accompanist to practice with these individuals. If the music minister does not come to the rehearsal to hear the musical offering, the accompanist is required to make difficult judgments regarding balance. This responsibility is one the accompanist may not enjoy. The music minister has arranged the musical selection, yet is not accepting musical responsibility. If a Sunday rehearsal is set for the music minister to hear the selection, the accompanist then must make necessary schedule adjustments.

An additional rehearsal right that an accompanist deserves is a tuned instrument. Regular tunings should be in the music budget as well as occasional "brush up" tunings. Nothing can destroy a choral sound like an out-of-tune instrument! The minister of music also needs to be certain that sight lines between the director and accompanist are clear. This may mean that a movement of the piano and/or director is necessary.

Recompense

An accompanist deserves appropriate recompense for skills that have been acquired in study, practice, and preparation. The minister of music should feel an obligation to the accompanist to see that these skills are rewarded sufficiently according to abilities, length of service, and duties. Too many personnel committees and music committees have no concept of the training and demands of the accompanist. The music minister may be concerned with the salary and benefits of his own position, yet it is also his or her duty to see that the accompanying position is financially supported. The accompanist's time is as valuable as that of the music minister. It is a well-known fact that pianists/organists in most churches must engage in many other paid jobs to support themselves financially.

Recognition

Recognition from the minister of music, the church, and committees is valuable for the accompanist, who is often the "unsung" musician of the church. The difference between an acceptable (even great) musical event and an unacceptable (hardly bearable) event sometimes lies in the hands of the accompanist. The music minister may have a choir with as many tenors as sopranos (is there such a choir?) and have difficulties with a choral selection being sung to its fullest intent due to an inadequate accompaniment. Conversely, there are many instances when the Sunday morning anthem or soloist has been saved by the musicianship and sensitivity of the accompanist. This reminds me of the story of the concertmaster of a symphony who, after having experienced great difficulty in following the direction of an inept guest conductor, declared to him in exasperation, "If you continue in this manner, we are really going to follow you!"

The music minister should be appreciative of the statement by Gerald Moore in *The Unashamed Accompanist*. He states, "Accompanying is an acquired art."[2] Moore, an unparalleled accompanist of the twentieth century, recognizes that the art of accompanying and ensemble playing "comes to one as the result of his experience, patience, and perseverance." Recognition of this ability from the minister of music toward the accompanist is a necessity for good teamwork.

Reciprocity

A dictionary definition of this word is "each to the other, mutual." There is a great need for reciprocity between accompanist and music minister. The accompanist can help the minister in many areas, often advising on matters of literature, choir personnel, community activities, etc. This is especially true of a new music minister in the church, when the accompanist has been a part of the church family for a period of time. They can be mutually helpful as plans are made for choir activities and church calendar.

The most valuable time when the music minister and the accompanist can be reciprocal is at a regular meeting set aside for planning and conversation. This meeting is best scheduled after the music minister has met with the pastor concerning services and activities. An hour is ideal, but even a half hour each week spent in talking mutually about upcoming events, choral literature, needs, and future services will accomplish much for the music ministry.

Another important reciprocal attitude for music minister and accompanist is respecting one another's time to prepare. An accompanist barging into the music minister's office without an appointment or prior notice disturbs study time or preparation. In like manner, when the accompanist is practicing for a service, the music minister should not interrupt. Reciprocal respect for practice, study, and office time between musicians goes a long way in a relationship.

The partnership between music minister and accompanist is a fifty-fifty affair. Respect, rehearsal rights, recompense, recognition, and reciprocity have been listed as essential for good relationships between ministers. There are many other "R's." These apply to the music minister as well as to the accompanist.

- Responsiveness. A query from either party deserves a ready response.
- Reconciliation. Problem arises need quick reconciliation.
- Remembrance. Birthdays and church anniversaries should be remembered.
- Resourcefulness. Effective service requires relying on each other.

The following "rights" were penned several years ago and are still applicable today.

The Accompanist's Right to Happiness

Inasmuch as the accompanist is the unsung hero of the choral art, it behooves all of us, in consideration of the unique and indispensable role played by accompanists everywhere, to extend every noble effort to enhance and enlarge on the state of happiness due such worthy practitioners of the music arts.

1. It shall be the right of every accompanist to have a well-tuned, high quality instrument on which to rehearse and perform. Such attention to mechanical detail benefits all.

2. In order to assist the musical programs to the utmost, the accompanist shall have the titles and sources for all hymns at least seven days in advance of their intended use.

3. It shall be the right of every accompanist to have in hand, three days before rehearsal, good clear copies of every anthem and other work to be rehearsed.

4. The provision of an accompanist's notebook, and a three-ring punch for material preparation shall be considered essential to the health, happiness, (and accuracy) of every accompanist.

5. In light of the need for absolute precision between director and accompanist, sightlines shall be as short as possible and absolutely uncluttered with either personnel, furniture, flowers, or other items that prevent visual communication.

6. Recognizing the colleague relationship between director and accompanist, it is essential that the accompanist be regarded by the church leadership as a staff member and that decisions involving music in any way shall be made known to the accompanist as soon as possible.

7. Since the skills involved in becoming a good accompanist are both of long preparation and of vast expense, it is essential that fair and adequate compensation be awarded for services rendered.

—adapted from *Hymn Playing Kit for Pianists* by Louis Ball

• *Mary Charlotte Ball is a retired associate professor of music at Carson-Newman College and has recently retired as the organist from First Baptist Church of Jefferson City, Tennessee, after thirty-eight years of service.*

REFERENCES

Harry Robert Wilson and Jack Lawrence Lyall, *Building a Church Choir* (Minneapolis: Hall & McCreary Company, 1957).

Gerald Moore, *The Unashamed Accompanist* (New York: MacMillan Company, 1956).

Louis Ball, *Hymn Playing Kit for Pianists* (Nashville, TN: Convention Press, 1979).

Ronald Allen and Gordon Borrer, *Worship* (Portland, OR: Multonomah, 1982).

Martin Thielen, *Getting Ready for Sunday—A Practical Guide for Worship Planning* (Nashville, TN: Broadman Press, 1989).

NOTES

[1] Harry Robert Wilson and Jack Lawrence Lyall, *Building a Church Choir* (Minneapolis: Hall & McCreary Company, 1957), 36.

[2] Gerald Moore, *The Unashamed Accompanist* (New York: MacMillan Company, 1956), vii.

Madeline Bridges

What the Minister of Music Needs to Know about Children's Choirs

Most pastors, church music committees, ministers of music, and church members agree that a comprehensive church music ministry should include children's choirs. However, the reasons used to defend the inclusion of such a program vary widely: "We need children to sing at Christmas." "We need a place for the children to go on Wednesday nights after dinner." "If the children sing in worship, their parents will come to our church service." "We need adult choir members in the future!"

It is difficult for ministers of music to develop a clear rationale regarding a children's music ministry until they understand "what" a church music program for children is or can be. This chapter begins with an overview of a children's choir ministry. Section 2 describes various aspects of planning and leading a rehearsal, and section 3 speaks directly to the responsibilities of the music minister in developing and maintaining a church music ministry for children. The chapter challenges ministers of music to develop and clearly articulate their personal set of beliefs about children's music ministry.

What Is a Children's Choir?

Who participates in a church music program for children? Children from age three through grade five or six (depending on the organization of the local school system) typically participate in children's choirs.

How many choirs are needed? The number of choirs varies from church to church. At the minimum, a church should provide a preschool choir (for four- and five-year-olds) and an elementary choir for grades 1-6. Dividing the elementary choir into a separate choir for lower elementary children (grades 1-3) and upper elementary children (grades 4-6) provides an even better environment for teaching and learning. In large churches, separate choirs for each grade level may be necessary.

When do children's choirs meet? Although a few choirs meet in the afternoon after school, most choir programs designate a time before or after a mid-week evening meal or service, during which all children's choirs meet simultaneously. The length of this designated time for children's choirs is typically forty to sixty minutes.

Who should lead a children's choir? The director of a children's choir should love children, understand music, and prepare with diligence for each rehearsal. In some church traditions, only trained music and music education professionals lead children's choirs. In other churches, while the oldest children's choir may be directed by a professionally trained musician, the leadership of other choirs is often provided by an interested, committed layperson. Many large churches appoint or hire a children's choir coordinator to recruit children and leaders, train and nurture leadership, order music and materials, and generally oversee the program. The music minister, however, remains a central element in the success of such a program.

What happens during a children's choir rehearsal? The content of children's rehearsals varies greatly with the age level of the choir as well as the performance expectations and worship style of the church. Children's choirs of all ages generally include—to a lesser or greater degree—the following kinds of experiences: learning and singing songs, anthems, and hymns; participating in rhythmic/moving/instrumental activities that often include some aspect of music reading; focus on worship education and ministry; and choir devotion. Many preschool and younger children's choir directors plan both large group activities (i.e., all children seated together in a group responding to the director) and small group activities (i.e., forming groups of five to eight children who work for ten to fifteen minutes with a choir assistant on a musical activity).

Goals of a Children's Choir Program

The church choir program must support the church as it expresses God's love to the world. It is essential that all aspects of the children's choir experience reflect the church and its teaching. If a children's choir looks, sounds, and feels exactly like a school music class or a community choir rehearsal, something vital is missing.

Hymns, songs, and anthems should comprise the bulk of the literature taught in a children's choir rehearsal. Additionally, fun songs, movement activities, and singing games are useful in teaching concepts and skills, and they also add variety to the rehearsal. Choir should aid the children in becoming more skillful singers, better music readers, and more knowledge-able about church music and worship.

Children's choirs must also teach the whole child, not just the child as future musician. Every aspect of the child—spiritual, physical, moral, intel-lectual, social, emotional—must be valued by those leading the choir. Church choirs must welcome every child regardless of the child's background or ability level. It is difficult to defend the inclusion of an auditioned chil-dren's choir in the church.

How Do Children Learn?

Children learn best when teaching is relevant. The methods and materials used in a children's choir must be developmentally appropriate to the age and maturity level of the child. It is beyond the scope of this chapter to delve deeply into the developmental characteristics of all ages, but the following characteristics of children are central:

• All children learn best by doing. They have relatively short attention spans and need frequent changes in rehearsal strategy. Preschool and younger children should not be expected to sit in rows for forty-five minutes and sing anthem after anthem like an adult choir. They function better if at least part of their rehearsal is structured as a small group experience. Many older children's choir directors also include small group activities in their rehearsals.

• Many children do not read with a high degree of proficiency and comfort until they are in the third grade. Most of the teaching of preschool and younger children will be by rote using pictures or short musical examples to aid their learning. An appropriate visual for preschoolers would be a picture cue for the four different verses of a song. Although older children can read and, with guidance, can follow a musical score, they also benefit from visuals.

• Children learn best when the learning environment is positive. When the learning environment is carefully structured and is led by confident, pre-pared teachers, children flourish. When chaos prevails, both children and leaders leave rehearsal with a sense of frustration. Children feel most posi-tively about choir when they feel they have been successful and yet challenged during the rehearsal. If everything is too hard, they are unable to feel successful and therefore do not leave choir with a positive feeling. If everything is too easy, they are bored. The choir environment should be one of joyful order.

What Should Happen During a Children's Choir Rehearsal?

A primary goal of children's choirs is to increase the singing skill of the children who come to choir. Singing is a highly valued part of worship, and choir should prepare children to participate in worship as part of a music ensemble or as a member of the congregation. Barring some physical disability, all children can increase their ability to sing tunefully. Time is of the essence. Concerned choir leaders are often the last people children encounter who care whether or not they can make a joyful noise in a tuneful manner.

Children's choir leaders must understand what it means for children to sing in their "head voice."[1] Directors need a clear mental model of head voice singing and must strive to help children achieve this sound. Head voice singing is healthy; it will give the child the ability to safely sing in *all* styles, and it will open the melodic range of children so they will not (as do so many adults) complain that songs and hymns are "too low." The goal of a church choir is not to reproduce the sound of an English boy-choir, but rather to give children the skills to sing freely and easily from their lower tones (near middle C) to their upper range.

Children singing in head voice do not look strained. Their voice quality tends to be clearer, and the volume level (at least initially) is quieter than the sound produced through chest voice singing. As children develop their head tone, however, they will delight in the strength and power of the upper register notes. Children's choir directors must understand that the inability of children to sing tunefully in the top half of the middle C octave is a clue, not that a child cannot sing or has a low range, but that the child is restricting himself or herself to singing in the chest register.

Much can be done in a children's choir rehearsal to foster this quality of sound. Consider the following suggestions:

• Choose songs and anthems that fall within the following melodic ranges:[2]
  Preschool: *d-b*
  Younger Children: *c-d2*
  Older Children: *B♭-g2*

• Regularly involve children in humorous vocal exploration games and exercises that take their voices high into the upper vocal register. Such activities (e.g., mimicking the melodic contour of a siren while singing an open-throated "whoo" sound) are typically brief, are perceived as a game, and often call on children to make sounds in their chest voice followed immediately by sounds in the upper register. An example of such an activity is to ask young children to say, "The sun is shining and I feel so fine" in a very low voice and immediately say it in a high voice like a mouse. Many older children's choir directors begin every rehearsal with vocal scoops and echoes that are far above the upper limits of range for song repertoire. Vocal exploration activities benefit the chronic underdeveloped singer who consistently does not sing on pitch as well as helping all singers find and strengthen their head voice register.

• Insist that children avoid using their "shouting" or "calling" voice when singing in choir. Some leaders find it useful to demonstrate the difference between a "calling voice," which is pitched, but which has a loud shouting quality, and the "singing voice," which is less strained and softer.

• Encourage children to sing more softly in their lower ranges but to use energy and sing with more intensity in their upper ranges. It is wise to avoid use of the words "sing louder" in rehearsals with children. Instead, encourage children to focus their sound on a particular spot, or ask them to "sing with more energy."

• Shy away from music for older children in which the melody consistently lies below "*a*." Such literature promotes chest voice singing.

Teaching Children to Sing . . . Beautifully

The children's choir director who wishes to help a children's choir sing more beautifully must base instruction on the same principles that form the foundation for beautiful singing in any choir. At any age, singing beautifully requires purposeful attention to *posture*, deep and controlling *breathing*, pure and consistent *vowel sounds*, clear and precise *consonants*, musical *phrasing*, and the subtleties of the *expressive qualities* of music (dynamics, tempo, and articulation). It is important that directors of children's choirs sing in a choir that encourages a high level of choral excellence.

The level of expectation in each of the areas mentioned above will increase as the child moves through a children's choir program. However, even preschoolers should "stand like singers" as they sing at least one song in every rehearsal. Younger children should learn about and begin to practice "singer's posture" and should learn to watch a director, sing with a dropped, relaxed jaw, and begin to add final consonants.

In choirs for older children, clear expectations for singing excellence should assume center stage. Children at this age want to be excellent. They are proud of their ability to sing a hymn descant. They respond to the challenge of holding their hymnals appropriately. They delight in the "*fl*" at the end of an anthem and will finish the word Lord with an accurate, concise voiced "*d*" if their choir director has prepared them well and conducts them with clarity.

Choir directors must take care to remember that their choristers are still children. They like challenge, but they want and need specific affirmation for their steps toward excellence. They are happier when they know the goals for a rehearsal and see their rehearsal progress in the form of an agenda. They need breaks from intense rehearsal in the form of a quick fun song. Children are concrete learners. For example, they respond quickly if the director holds a light bulb beside the face (socket end near the mouth) to encourage children to visualize the abstract concept of "opening the back of the throat."

Knowing children and searching for ways to present singing concepts in a childlike manner is vital, but it is equally important to hold high expectations of these choristers. As an experienced mentor once told this author, "Children in older children's choir can sing anything you can teach them, and they can and will sing at any level of musicianship toward which you are willing to strive."

Choosing Music

Although worship styles and traditions vary, the following guidelines regarding music choices are valid for all children's music programs:

- *Text.* Choose music with a text children can understand. Make the music worth the time and energy the choir will expend in learning it. Texts from Scripture are always appropriate. Remember that children also respond well to imaginative texts and to texts in other languages.

- *Melodic and rhythmic content.* Choose songs and anthems that fall within the guidelines for melodic range and tessitura presented earlier in this chapter. Songs in which the melody moves primarily by large intervals are more difficult than songs that use a predominance of step-wise movement. When considering an anthem, directors should sing the melody and note whether it is a singable tune. Some anthems with more challenging melodies are worth the extra effort; others are not. Choose wisely. Consider the key and the meter of the anthem in contrast with other music in the choir's folder. Singing every song in 6/8 meter in the key of F can result in a musically boring rehearsal!

• *Harmony.* Developing a tuneful, accurate unison sound should be the primary goal of a children's choir program. However, directors of older children's choirs should also provide opportunities for choristers to experience singing in harmony. A choir's ability to sing in harmony will develop more quickly and thoroughly if the director begins a logical progression to true soprano-alto harmony, which includes experiences in the following:
> —Solid, confident unison singing
> —Partner songs or anthems that combine two familiar melodies
> —Choral ostinatos (repeated patterns) that accompany a melody
> —Rounds/canons
> —Countermelodies or descants
> —Alto harmony that moves mostly in thirds and sixths with the melody
> —True, independent alto part

• *Form.* Verse-refrain anthems, hymn anthems, and anthems organized in a clear three-part form (ABA) or in rondo form (ABACADA) can be learned more quickly than lengthy through-composed anthems. However, the length of text rather than the length of the anthem itself is the factor that most directly affects how long it takes a choir to learn an anthem. Utilize the anthem's form as an aid to memorization, and help children understand that composers use form to organize their compositions.

• *Vocal considerations. Tessitura,* the average range of pitches in a musical composition, is the prime factor in whether or not a choir can sing an anthem beautifully. If the melody lies too low, the choir will tend to sing in an unmusical, chest-voice manner. Directors should also look carefully at high, sustained pitches in the anthem. If the vowel sounds on such pitches are AH, OH, or OO, the choir will be much more successful than trying to sustain an EE or EH on a high pitch. Phrase length is another important vocal consideration. It is possible to teach an older children's choir to stagger-breathe, but the task is not easy. Attempting to sustain lengthy phrases often results in loss of energy and in pitch problems at the end of the phrase. Choosing to add a musical breath in the middle of a long phrase (even if there is not a comma) is often a logical decision.

• *Additional Guidelines:*
    —Avoid choosing music because "it's a cute piece."
    —Decide whether or not the choir has *time* to learn the piece. If the anthem has many appealing qualities, but the time line is short, consider leaving out a portion of the anthem, doubling a part on an instrument, using a soloist or small ensemble on one section or stanza, or having another choir sing part of the anthem.
    —Select anthems that can involve more than one choir. Presenting a multi-choir anthem in the context of a worship service is invigorating for the congregation and the singers.
    —Choose anthems that fit the pedagogical needs of the choir program. Ask, "What will the children know—about music, about their faith, and about worship—after they learn this anthem?"
    —Before ordering an anthem, sing it aloud and determine whether or not it is interesting and singable.
    —Regardless of the musical style of the anthem, look for music that is well-crafted and avoids musical and textural clichés.

Teaching Musical Concepts

Many children's choir directors ask, "When do I teach music theory?" Although a few choir programs work methodically through a theory workbook, most children's choir directors choose to incorporate music reading into repertoire rehearsal. Memorizing lines and spaces on the staff has little value unless the children are actively involved in singing intervals, playing instruments, and relating their learning directly to the songs and anthems they sing.

Often, young choirs are taught using a strategy sometimes referred to as the "rote-note" method. For example, even though younger elementary children learn songs primarily by ear, the wise director will select and extract a few measures of the song and use the melodic or rhythmic pattern to strengthen the music reading skills of the children. Children's choir programs should have specific music reading goals for each choir and should plan for children to exit the choir program with (1) the ability to successfully follow a musical score, (2) an understanding of basic rhythmic and melodic notation, and (3) a basic knowledge of music vocabulary.

Educating Children about Worship and Their Church Music Heritage

Children's choirs should reinforce and strengthen their church's worship and music tradition. Churches that follow the liturgical year often weave discussion of the liturgical seasons into choir activities. All churches can help children understand that singing has been a part of worship since Old Testament days. Children's choirs also reinforce the importance of music in the Christian life in today's society. Informing and involving children in worship education strengthens their understanding of music in worship and equips them to participate more fully as a worship participant for the rest of their lives.

No aspect of church music education for children is more important than providing opportunities for children to increase their repertoire of hymns, their understanding of the important role of hymnody in the Christian tradition, and their knowledge about hymn writers. Other than the Bible, the hymnal is the most important source of Christian truths. Even pastors admit that most congregants can quote more hymn stanzas than Scripture or sermons. A hymn memory program is an important part of many children's choirs. When children are able to see a connection between the hymns sung in worship and their hymn study in choirs, they grow in their love and appreciation of hymnody.

Planning for Children's Participation in Worship

The frequency with which children's choirs participate in public worship varies widely. The minister of music and children's choir leadership must come to a clear and careful understanding regarding expectations for children's participation in worship.

Forcing preschoolers to stand in rows and sing an anthem (as an older children's choir would do) is contrary to their physical and emotional developmental level. Such a presentation inadequately represents the essence of the preschool choir experience. However, hosting a choir open house once or twice a year offers a wonderful chance for parents and friends to see the variety of musical activities children experience each week. Parents can watch as preschoolers sing songs, play instruments, create their own music, participate in music and singing games, and hear stories about Bible musicians.

In most churches, younger children's choirs sing in worship at least once a semester, and older children's choirs often participate in worship every four to six weeks. Ministers of music who purposefully involve the children's choirs in meaningful worship leadership (not simply putting on a show) will strengthen the understanding of everyone—children's choir directors, the children themselves, parents, and members of the congregation—about the appropriate role of children in worship.

Children's choirs often learn and present a musical each year. When carefully chosen, a musical can be meaningful both to participants and to the congregation. Consider rehearsing and presenting a musical in a summer music camp setting. Scheduling in this manner allows the limited weekly rehearsal time during the year to be reserved for learning anthems, strengthening singing skills, learning to read music, hymn study, and worship education.

Using Curriculum Materials for Children's Choir

Publishers now offer several types of resources—not simply octavos—for use in children's choir programs. Choristers Guild, a national membership organization, publishes an outstanding bimonthly magazine for leadership of children's and youth choirs titled *The Chorister*.[3] The periodical includes feature articles relating to the field of church music for children and youth, reviews of choral music for these ages, choir devotions, practical suggestions for choir rehearsals, hymn studies, and ideas for promoting and recruiting children. Additionally, a membership in Choristers Guild provides the member with sample copies (typically three to five each month) of all new choral publications for children and youth.

Several sources also publish curriculum for use in children's choirs. The most widely used curricula are briefly described below:

- *Church Music for Children,* published by Abingdon Press,[4] is a three-year children's choir curriculum for four different age levels: pre-elementary, younger elementary, older elementary, and combined elementary children.

- LifeWay Christian Resources[5] publishes a widely used curriculum and other music resources for use in children's choirs. For each level—preschool, younger children, and older children—a set of material is available for leaders and children. For example, the core resources recommended for use with older children include *Young Musicians*—a magazine for older children that includes a music insert of songs and anthems for this age chorister—and *Young Musicians Pak* (including a teacher's guide; compact disc recording of songs in *Young Musicians*; charts, posters, games, and other resource material; and an instructional video).

• Musikgarten[6] publishes a resource titled *Music and Movement: God's Children Sing*. The book includes 200 activities for use in a Judeo-Christian tradition church music program. This curriculum is organized according to potential activities and features weekly formats.

• *Stepping Stones* (published by Choristers Guild) is a three-year sequential children's choir curriculum. Within each year, there are two levels—one for early childhood and one for early elementary. Apart from the three-year sequence, the series also includes a separate book for older elementary children. The curriculum is based on Kodaly methodology and the liturgical year, and it makes significant use of teaching the hymns during choir rehearsal.

What Is the Responsibility of the Music Minister?

The music minister is the key to a successful children's music ministry. If the church's primary music leader values the children's choir experience for the church, the program can flourish. Ministers of music must be convinced that children's choirs make a difference in the lives of the children and in the life of the church. They must realize that the future of the church music program rests on the firm foundation children receive in a comprehensive children's choir program. They must value the week-by-week content of children's choir rehearsals.

Ministers of music must understand that children learn by doing; they must recognize and affirm appropriate singing habits in children. They must know that preschoolers have different musical, social, and educational needs than sixth graders. They must strive to maintain challenging yet realistic musical goals for the children's choir program. If possible, music ministers should direct (or help lead) a children's choir. At the least, they must stay involved in the program and join choir leaders as they learn how to do their job in the most effective way possible.

Recruit Leadership

Recruiting children's choir directors and assistants is an important task for the music minister. Look for leaders who are active in the church music ministry. Identify adults and older youth who care about children. Ask about church members who have music education backgrounds and may have taught public school music. Do not be afraid to choose assistants—and even directors for younger choirs—who may not have extensive musical backgrounds. It is important that all potential musical leaders for children's choirs love children, have a pleasant and appropriate singing voice, and indicate willingness to learn and be trained.

Provide Leadership Training

The music minister should coordinate training for the children's choir leadership in many areas, including singing, conducting, accompanying, methods and materials for use in the children's choir, understanding children and how they learn, the unique challenges of working with the child's voice, and developing appropriate discipline strategies for choir. Training may occur as a workshop in the local church, or the music minister may arrange for children's choir leaders to attended local, regional, or national conferences. Always look for material that may be helpful to the choir leaders, including instructional videos.

Budget for Children's Choirs

A children's music ministry's budgetary needs are multifaceted. In addition to funds for purchasing multiple copies of anthems, a comprehensive children's choir program needs a designated budget for instruments, curriculum materials, compact disc recordings of excellent children's choirs, folders, food and decorations for social events, expendable material such as construction paper and markers, audiovisual equipment such as an overhead projector and "boom boxes," and costumes for musical presentations.

Nurture and Encourage Children's Choir Leadership

Few children's choir leaders feel overly appreciated! An important responsibility of the minister of music is to nurture and encourage leaders of the children's music ministry. This encouragement should take many forms, but it should always include public and private verbal affirmation of dedicated choir leaders. A choir teacher or assistant is usually delighted when the minister of music takes the time to come to all or part of a rehearsal. Personal notes that specifically praise or comment on some aspect of the rehearsal are meaningful. Many ministers of music plan an end-of-the year dinner or open house to express publicly the church's appreciation to its music leadership.

Coordinate Schedule

The music minister is vitally involved with children's choir in the scheduling of choir rehearsals, the beginning and end of the choir year, times for children's choirs to participate in worship, opportunities for the children's choir to sing a multi-choir anthem with the adult choir, major church music events such as the hanging of the green service in which children may participate, and training events for leadership. Remember to be flexible and responsive to requests from a children's choir director who asks to reschedule a date for a choir to sing because the children are simply not yet ready.

Conclusion

Perhaps the most important responsibility for ministers of music is to develop and confidently express their own personal philosophy of church music education for children. This set of beliefs should express feelings about and understanding of music and its role in the church, children and how children learn, the role of the children's choir in the church music program, the important responsibilities of children's music leadership, the contribution of choir experience to a child's life and future, and what should be taught and learned within a children's choir program.

A strongly worded, firmly grounded set of beliefs about a children's music ministry will serve for the duration of the ministry. When ministers of music know what they believe about this important aspect of music ministry, they will find it easier to shape their actions based on these beliefs. When circumstances become difficult, a confident set of beliefs will allow the music minister to hold true to the course.

The ultimate fruits of a children's choir ministry may surface in another church at another time and place. However, it is clear that the potential benefit of positive, expressive, and disciplined children's choir participation is unlimited. Being nurtured by a church ministry that includes a strong children's choir program will contribute directly to a child's musical, spiritual, and character development. As the world grows more and more complex, the music minister, the children's choir leadership, and the local church must join hands to meet the challenge. Children deserve our best efforts. Nothing less is sufficient.

• *Madeline Bridges* *is professor of music at Belmont University and teaches in the area of music education. She co-directs the Nashville Children's Choir and has an extensive background in children's choirs.*

REFERENCES

Mary DeLaine Allcock and Madeline Bridges, *How to Lead Children's Choirs* (Nashville, TN: Convention Press, 1988). Printed on demand by LifeWay Christian Resources.

Rhonda Edge and Barbara Sanders, *How to Lead Preschoolers in Musical Activities* (Nashville TN: Convention Press, 1988). Printed on demand by LifeWay Christian Resources.

Helen Kemp, *Of Primary Importance* (Garland, TX: Choristers Guild; vol. 1 [1988)], vol. 2 [1991]).

Shirley McRae, *Directing the Children's Choir: A Comprehensive Resource* (New York: Schirmer Books, 1991).

Linda Swears, *Teaching the Elementary School Chorus* (West Nyack, NY: Parker Publishing Company, 1985).

John D.Witvliet, ed., *A Child Shall Lead: Children in Worship—A Sourcebook for Christian Educators, Musicians, and Clergy* (Garland, TX: Choristers Guild, 1999).

NOTES

[1] "Head voice" and "chest voice" are terms used to describe opposite ways of producing a sound. Other frequently-used designations include "upper mechanism and "lower mechanism."

[2] This chapter refers to middle C and the pitches in the octave above middle C as *c, d,* etc. Pitches in the next highest octave are designated *c1, c2,* etc. Pitches in the octave below middle C are designated by capital letters.

[3] For additional information about *The Chorister,* Choristers Guild membership, or anthems/curriculum materials published by Choristers Guild, email choristers@choristers-guild.org or call 972-271-1521.

[4] For additional information about Abington Press publications for children, call 1-800-672-1789.

[5] For additional information about music resources for children published by LifeWay Christian Resources, call 1-800-436-3869.

[6] For additional information regarding this publication, contact Music Matters, Inc., 1-800-216-6864.

John Simons

Working with Middle School Church Choirs

One of my colleagues mused, "For every complex problem, there is usually a simple solution and it is usually wrong." There are no easy solutions or models that "always work" concerning middle school music ministry. Each ministry is unique and soars or falls dependent on the leader's philosophy, information, and connection. Philosophy forms the foundation and creates a plan for a dynamic ministry. Information helps the church musician develop the limitless potential God gave middle school students and expands the leader's ability to imagine and dream. Connection provides the tools needed for renewal, helps the conductor deal with the fluid nature of middle school ministry, and allows the created ministry to progress beyond the limitations of human leadership.

Philosophy

Do middle school students have a place in your philosophy of ministry? Through observation and empirical data, the conclusion is that middle school and high school youth are different. However, few church musicians develop a ministry plan to address the needs of middle school students.

In developing a program that includes middle school students, the conductor has to eliminate the thought that the problem is the middle school child or the maturation process. Trying to make middle school students model adult behavior is as futile as ignoring puberty. The core hindrance is not youth behavior or issues of growing up, but church musicians who fail to understand their influence on adolescent youth. They exchange opportunities for life-changing ministry with matters of convenience, poorly conceived definitions of discipline, or temporary success.

Imagine an ideal ministry tailor-made for your situation. Stephen Covey states, "Begin with an end in mind."[1] Allow time to meditate and dream about the fully developed ministry. What does it look like? How does it minister to the children and community? Where does it fit in the general music ministry and life of the church? What are the personal costs in running the ministry? Why do students participate in the ministry? Clarify what you want to create.

The principle is that things are created in the mind before they are created in physical form. By recognizing the reality of a situation, we see alternative choices and avoid draining existing areas of critical resources. Create a mission based on your visualized ministry and plan by priorities. The priorities depend on the level of information you gather about a subject and the imagined product.

I have observed and experienced middle school church music ministry created without vision. In most cases, the group dissolves due to lack of focus, disbands after the original leader leaves, fails to secure financial support, falls short of the singers' expectations, or overworks the leader to the point of exhaustion. Most leaders have made this mistake and try to avoid repeating it. Before moving to the next section, answer this question: Are middle school youth important enough to give the time and energy required? As you consider your answer, do not limit the results of your choice to the creation of a choir. Perhaps your situation calls for a strategic plan to work with the young singers outside of the rehearsal, to rewrite parts to make SATB music fit the needs of adolescent voices, or to listen to your middle school students with empathy rather than apathy.

Dream about the ultimate product and plan backward from the current situation. As you focus on what you can do, plan using foundational principles that create areas of priority. Define the mission and begin the journey.

Information

Collecting information concerning adolescent qualities and vocal needs will aid in the development of an effective middle school ministry plan. This section begins with a brief discussion of adolescent behavior characteristics, moves to a discussion of the vocal areas taught to both girls and boys, and concludes with the leading theories concerning the changing voice. If you are unfamiliar with the similarities and differences in the Royal School of Church Music, Continental, or North American approaches to the child's voice, please refer to the chapter dealing with children's choirs and study any number of books concerning vocal pedagogy for children.

Adolescent Qualities

There are three basic adolescent qualities to consider when working with middle school singers: peer acceptance, energy plus, and fun. Peer acceptance is a major consideration. Adolescent children are more likely to be influenced by their peers than by their adult leaders. As you plan and dream, consider creating an environment in which each youth is accepted. The group pressure and example will filter into every aspect of your ministry, and the minister of music can direct this quality to a positive outcome.

Energy plus is a fact: middle schoolers have more energy than you. Instead of fighting this quality, channel it. Build elements into your rehearsal and ministry that allow them to express themselves with physical movement and other spontaneous activities. Using your creativity, make quality fun. Instead of fighting their natural "silliness," put it to positive use. Allow time for laughter and fun activities, but insist on quality and rehearsal etiquette. Use games and physical activity in the rehearsal to keep the pace fast. Middle school students are neither children nor adults, and they are moving from concrete to abstract thinkers. Once inspired, they are relentless in the pursuit of a goal and enjoy the synergy created by group interaction.

Boys and Girls Together: Common Vocal Needs

Boys and girls develop in significantly different ways during puberty. When working with this obvious fact, conductors seem to focus on the differences. Since boys and girls rehearse together in most youth choir programs, church musicians need to study the basic techniques common to both groups. This subsection presents aspects of vocal pedagogy that need to be taught to middle school boys and girls. Ken Phillips identifies five basic areas common to both male and female adolescent vocal development: proper breathing, phonation, resonant tone production, diction, and expression. I add posture to this list. If you make vocal development a high priority, so will your middle school singers.

Breathing is bimodal. The first mode is chest breathing. Place your hands on your chest and breathe toward your hands (first mode). This type of breathing is used to quickly move oxygen to the bloodstream. Intense physical activity is associated with this type of breathing. The second mode uses the area associated with the diaphragm. Place your hands just below your sternum and breathe toward your hands (second mode). This type of breathing is used to sustain long periods of physical activity and control. Singing uses the second mode of breath management and forms the foundation for the consistency of air pressure needed to sustain pitch, control auditory volume, and produce a healthy vocal tone.

Phonation deals with the way the vocal folds vibrate to make sound and involves registers. In phonation, there are three steps: attack, sustentation, and release. A good attack is a mental and physical process. One must think before adjusting the muscular action necessary to begin sound. In dealing with middle school youth, this can be a challenge. The sustentation of sound usually relates to breath management, and the important aspect is the consistency of the sound from the attack to the release. The release is a coordinated movement between the articulators, breath, and vocal chords. In working with middle school youth, help them avoid "pinching" the release by bringing the vocal folds together to stop the airflow. Instead rely on the articulators. When releasing on a vowel sound, release it as if it had a final consonant.

Registers are identified by the different vibratory patterns of the vocal folds within a range of produced pitches. Unfortunately, there are as many opinions concerning registers as there are terms to identify various registers. Theories range from four separate distinct registers to one seamless register. I hold to a three-register concept identified as high, middle, and low.

Common practice in developing strategies to cover the breaks between the registers is to work from the upper register down to the other registers. Practitioners observe that most singers are able to mix the registers more effectively when moving high to low. The singer is able to maneuver low to high with efficiency after they learn to mix high to low. This helps teach boys who want to sing in a forced lower register. For girls, exploration of the upper register brings elements of clarity and ring to the breathy quality of the middle register and pressed quality of the lower register.

Resonant tone production concerns the "space" used to create sound. The position involves a gentle lift to the soft palate while relaxing the pharynx wall, and an awareness of the position of the larynx during phonation. In working with middle school singers, the position of the larynx tends to migrate up as the pitch rises. For resonant tone production, the larynx should be at a low position. Keeping the larynx in an "at rest" position is a mental awareness element of singing rather than a physical manipulation technique.

Diction involves the manipulation of the articulators (tongue, lips, jaw, teeth) and teaching lyric pronunciation of texts. Choral ensembles must utilize vowel unification and consonant articulation to be understood. As you teach middle school singers, use musical terms and proper muscular descriptions. Consider teaching singers the International Phonetic Alphabet (IPA) and build on their natural tendency to explore, learn, and demonstrate knowledge. Make students aware of the difference between spoken language and sung language.

One word of caution: church musicians should not expect middle school students to warm to exercises involving physical contact. However, group activities (non-touching), private study, and self-awareness exercises work well with this age. When teaching activities or new skills, remember that middle school students go through a mental process, physical process, and emotional process. Be patient. Changing poor vocal technique takes time, and overlooking emotional aspects will add time and frustration to the change.

Expressiveness is difficult to teach. Communications experts suggest that 10 percent of our communication is represented by the words we say, 30 percent by our sounds, and 60 percent by our body language. Since a major element of communication deals with body language, this presents an obstacle for middle school students who are overly aware of their physical changes. Understanding this element helps the church musician develop communication skills and design activities to communicate meaning and expressiveness. As you teach the expressive quality of a musical phrase, couple it with a group movement. This will help the students understand the nature of the phrase and help you assess their understanding of the concept. Think of the power of physical actions in worship and transfer that information to communication in rehearsals. Use nonverbal games or even try a "silent" rehearsal where the only sounds made are singing. Help the students explore communicating through facial expressions, posture, body position, and movement.

Correct posture allows the body to function at optimal ability. For singing, use the term *ki-position*. "Ki" is a term taken from the martial art *akito* and refers to the body being in a position of balance—weight evenly distributed on the balls of the feet, feet shoulder-width apart, legs relaxed with a slight bend in the knees, back straight with a slight feeling of lift to the spinal column, chest comfortably high, shoulders square and slightly rolled back, arms at the side with no tension in the hands, and head in line with the body. When singing seated, keep the back off the chair, both feet on the floor (no crossed legs), and the rest is the same as standing. Middle school students enjoy playing posture games. It may be useful to try hand signals to tell them to go to seated position, standing position, or relaxed position. This is also good for a physical warm-up at the beginning of a rehearsal.

These common elements form the foundation of teaching middle school students to express their faith through choral music making. Notice that style is not an issue. Choose literature appropriate for their physical, mental, spiritual, and emotional levels, and teach good vocal habits regardless of style. In selecting quality literature, consider the appropriateness of the text, the tessitura of the parts, and the vocal/communication skills needed to make the piece an expressive work of art. When working in rehearsal, evaluate your communication skills to see if you teach these foundational elements in each rehearsal.

The Changing Male Voice

Males tend to enter puberty between ages twelve and fourteen. The larynx grows laterally and anteriorly, and the vocal folds lengthen an average of ten to eleven millimeters. Psychologically, they are dealing with a deeper level of understanding and awareness of self. Physically, the rapid growth and hormonal changes make any skill based on muscular coordination difficult to master. The combination of the mental and physical aspects of singing makes mastery or even enjoyment of the skill problematic for the adolescent singer.

A number of theories have been advanced about the male changing voice. Irving Cooper and his disciple, John Cooksey, did the most convincing recent work. Cooper presented ideas that spawned the Cambiata Concept. The concept is that boys singing throughout vocal mutation assist the eventual settling process of the voice and contribute to artistic expression as long as they sing music written for their range and tessitura. Range is the distance between their lowest and highest notes, and tessitura is the practical singing range. His ideas allowed boys to sing during their vocal mutation without compromising musical or artistic standards. The word *cambiata* became the term most identified with boys going through the vocal change. Cooper believed that 90 percent of boys go through the vocal mutation process in a predictable manner: in general, soprano to cambiata in the seventh grade, moving to baritone in the eighth grade. The lower voices then developed in ninth grade, and real tenors developed sometime later. Cooper's ideas continue to be developed today through his disciples, the Cambiata Vocal Music Institute of America, Inc. founded by Don Collins, and the music publications of Cambiata Press. Cooper gave four classifications for male singers during adolescence: (1) unchanged/sopranos, (2) first phase/cambiata, (3) second phase/baritone, (4) changed basses. Cooper encourages the choir to sing in parts due to the difficulty of finding melodies that have a common tessitura. In addition, he tells the students what is happening and how the classifications work. This takes the mystery out of the process and sets up an expectation that the boys will move through a process without losing face or becoming an irrelevant part of the ensemble. In adopting the cambiata concept, repertoire becomes a major issue. Cooper strongly opposed assigning the cambiata voices to either the tenor or alto parts in standard SATB literature. He cautioned the use of SAB literature for the same reasons. Instead, he suggested and helped develop music specifically designed for the cambiata voice: SAC and SACT/B music. In all cases, he stressed the absolute need to remember tessitura, text, and techniques when selecting repertoire.[2]

The Contemporary Eclectic Theory took the Cambiata Concept to a more complex level of detail. John Cooksey, a student of Cooper, developed and presented a practical approach to working with young singers supported by an impressive body of research. In brief, he expanded the cambiata approach from two phases of change to three phases of change called midvoice I (initial period of voice change), midvoice II (high mutational period), and midvoice IIA (climax of mutation and key transition period).[3]

As with the Cambiata Concept, the Contemporary Eclectic Theory supports the use of music specifically designed for each level of maturation. Cooksey has taken an aggressive approach to training teachers and tirelessly promotes the benefits of working with the changing voice. Teachers are admonished not to exercise register extremes in either direction, but rather to exercise the changing voices within their comfortable tessitura. This presents a serious problem for the church musician. Literature matching the specific needs of the three types of changing voice is difficult to find, and training musicians to correctly classify the three stages of change is somewhat problematic. However, Cooksey's research contributes to understanding the detailed and complex nature of the vocal change. An interesting result of his studies is in the area of predicting voice classification. He asserts there is some evidence to support claims that voices that mature early/quickly will become basses and those that mature late/slowly will become high baritones or tenors.

For church music, the author supports a blend of the above approaches combined with Sally Herman's Voice-Pivot Approach. Each theory has merit, but the time restrictions placed on the church youth choir are a serious concern. The normal church youth choir meets for fifty minutes once a week. Holding to the tradition of developing the high, middle, and low registers in a child's voice, the church musician can immediately begin to develop all the registers in the changing and changed voices. Cultivate the upper register and middle register during the vocal mutation and begin exploring the lower male register as the voice settles. Using Herman's approach, the cambiata voices sing elements of different voice parts within a musical piece. They "pivot" from one vocal part to the next to account for range and tessitura. Blend and balance issues should be handled with care, but the singer is allowed to remain in his comfortable singing range throughout an SATB piece. As with all the theories, it requires the conductor to know the voices within the choir and track the progress of the mutational stages of each singer.

Here are a few suggestions to church musicians based on these theories. Avoid SAB and unison literature because of range and tessitura issues. When weaning a choir from unison music, begin with canons and move to two parts. When they can sing two parts, move them to three, then four parts. As voices change, move the singers to the appropriate voice parts. Do not make an issue of moving singers to the appropriate voice part; make it a normal part of choir rehearsal. When boys do not want to sing in their high register, yet their voices have not changed, the church musician must explain the changes that are going to happen and help the singer understand that the vocal folds are muscles that need to be worked in a proper manner. Treat the vocal change and the stages of change as normal, and do not make fun or allow others to make fun of the boys going through vocal mutation. Although some of the theories support working the extremities of the registers, none of the theories support forcing the changing voice to sing music out of its core sound. Try not to underestimate the singers' ability to maintain standards and adapt to the supportive environment in a rehearsal. Finally, learn from mistakes.

The Female Changing Voice

This is a new area of serious study. Recent research indicates that American females are entering puberty at age ten or eleven instead of twelve to fourteen. This poses new problems for middle school church music leaders. Medically, female vocal folds lengthen about three to four millimeters during puberty. As the mutation occurs, you will notice some uneasiness in the speaking voice, but mostly it can be heard in the increased breathiness in the vocal tone. The range of the upper register decreases during the period of mutation. Girls' voices move from a flute-like quality to a more "husky" tone. Unfortunately, this is how many females are misclassified as altos. Once the girls move through the mutation process, their voice settles and the upper register returns with a more resonant tone. To strengthen the musculature, most vocal pedagogues encourage exercising the upper register and discourage the development of an unnatural chest or lower register quality.

Lynne Gackle has emerged as the leading expert on the adolescent female voice. She suggests nine indicators to help musicians diagnose the changing female voice: insecurity of pitch; development of register breaks; increased huskiness in the voice; decreased and inconsistent range capabilities; voice cracking; lowering of speaking voice; uncomfortable singing or difficulty in phonation; heavy, breathy, rough tone production or thin tone quality; unexplained hoarseness.

Her theory asserts four stages of development. The prepubertal stage is characterized by a light, flute-like quality with no real register breaks. The pubescent/premenarcheal stage involves increased breathiness in the vocal quality, difficulty in achieving volume in the upper and middle register, and the appearance of the low or chest register. In the puberty/postmenarcheal stage, hoarseness occurs without any upper respiratory or cheerleading problems, girls lack clear tone quality, the tessitura fluctuates, and distinct register breaks between the upper-middle and middle-lower registers are apparent. The young adult female stage has an increased range, richer tone, less breathiness as the mutational chink closes, and an ease returning to the ability to sing.[4]

Most vocal experts agree that one should not classify adolescent female voices as either soprano or alto. Instead, treat them as evenly divided soprano parts and do not abuse their voices by selecting music that exploits the extreme lows or highs of their range. As with the male changing voice, work the voice from high to low rather than low to high. Consider using words such as full instead of loud, pure instead of soft, and understand that the attitude of the singer is a relevant issue.

The changing voice (male and female) is an enormous subject and a specialized area of study. The information in this section was given in brief form. As you work with middle school voices, take time to read the research from primary source areas. As students move through stages of mutation, the eventual settling of the voice will not occur during the middle school years. Classifications such as baritone or soprano should be thought of in the context of the middle school range and tessitura.

Connection

Connection is often overlooked in the training of most church musicians. One can have a solid philosophy, know all the information concerning the adolescent voice, select quality literature, and fail miserably because of a lack of connection. The idea of connection is central in assisting middle school students to express their faith, emotions, and thoughts. This section will present personality traits of successful middle school musicians, discuss renewal, and give suggestions for working with the middle school culture. Since you cannot control the actions of others, be concerned with your connections: musician to student, musician to musician, and musician to parent.

Musician to Student

Making a connection with students begins with the leader. Middle school ministry leaders must be confident in their skills, secure in their personal relationships, comfortable with themselves, and sincere in their faith. The following is a selected list of traits demonstrated by people successfully working with middle school singers. The observations are from the author's experience combined with the observations of Anthony Barresi: passion, spiritual maturity, commitment to youth, maintaining a healthy adult-to-child relationship, having a sense of humor without sarcasm, communication skills, creativity, problem solving, lifelong learner, and belief in the free sharing of information and the refinement of ideas.[5]

Although adolescents are more apt to be influenced by their peers, the modeling of healthy personal habits in a welcoming environment cannot be understated. Young singers will follow your standards. Notice that the profile does not include traits like excellent entertainer, kid at heart, ball of energy, etc. These traits can be beneficial, but they are not an indicator of success.

Church musicians tend to possess most of the qualities in the profile of successful middle school leaders. Middle school students are exploring behavior and humor. Beyond bathroom humor, they explore sarcasm. Eventually, cutting remarks lose their sarcastic allure and become hurtful. Girls and boys enter into this type of harmful communication with equal vigor, and ministers who adopt a kid-at-heart or manipulative attitude do great harm to the real emotional feelings of middle school students. Think about how we communicate using humor, and understand the far-reaching extent of your influence.

Communication goes beyond organizational skills, and motivating the singers is often tied to the minister's ability to communicate vision and expectations. Since middle school students are moving from concrete thought to abstract thought, they desire to explore and demonstrate their capabilities. Communication with middle school students should be synergistic. Listen with an empathetic ear, take their suggestions seriously, and help them open their minds to new possibilities. Most creative endeavors involve an element of unpredictability with trial-and-error experiences. In planning a musical event, I form my middle school youth choir into four groups: script, choreography, sets, sound/light technology. The groups meet before the choral rehearsals. The levels of energy and involvement of the students in such circumstances have overwhelmed me. The choreography takes new life, and those who take dance are giddy with excitement at the application of their area in a worship context. The technically savvy kids plot the light and sound guides for the show, the literal-minded students reshape outdated scripts and made them relative to their experience, and the hands-on students discover the beauty of light-weight flats, Styrofoam™, and water-based paints. The process can be chaotic, takes a long time, sometimes involves complaining parents, and includes many failures on the road to the final product. Supervision is often difficult, and giving directions and "reality" checks are time-consuming. However, the performance becomes something relevant, dynamic and powerful. Synergy, creativity, and open communication are exciting aspects of life that can be modeled effectively at the middle school level.

Instead of being tied to the latest product, connect to your singers and create your own music. Teach the young girls how to use their full vocal ranges instead of the lower or chest register utilized by pop singers. If they are inspired and moved by that style of music, at least teach them to perform it in a non-damaging way. Through connection and using your knowledge, help middle school youth explore alternative possibilities. If vocal health is a point of connection, your repertoire selections will reveal your beliefs.

Musician to Musician

One of the most progressive groups in the country concerning youth choir is YouthCue, Inc. Their success lies in high-quality national festivals and their connectional system of church musicians. It is synergistic, creative, and revolutionary. Ideas are freely exchanged via email, people share problems and solutions via a newsletter, and annual roundtable discussions are conducted throughout the United States. Randy Edwards, founder of YouthCue, states four reasons youth participate in youth choir: spiritual, musical, emotional, and social.[6] Using these four elements, a music minister can create a set of values to help guide his or her program. As you envision and plan a middle school ministry, list the elements of your plan divided into these four areas. It will help balance values and reveal areas of concern.

Since the energy level of middle school youth goes beyond adult capabilities, burnout and fatigue are serious issues. Most of my church music colleagues wait until they are at a breaking point before seeking renewal. My colleagues who continue to minister well beyond the start-up phase of a ministry consistently seek renewal. They attend seminars, take their day off, join connectional groups of ministers, and focus on areas of integrity, relationship, and personal health. They model a healthy spiritual life, family life, and love of life. Instead of being bored or crisis-oriented, they are full of ideas and look forward to the challenges of a new day.

Musician to Parent

The middle school culture is market-driven. One look at MTV reveals the success of market strategy in shaping the definition of "cool." Connection is the tool used to achieve this obvious and dangerous business success. Why discuss middle school culture in a section titled "musician to parent"? It is not to relay the obvious organizational information about the importance of mail-outs, parent meetings, web-based information pages, tour books, etc. It is to relay an overlooked reality: you are not the students' parent. Their parents are the ones charged with the task of raising them. Church musicians are not trained family counselors or child psychologists. Complex problems should be referred to trained counselors, and middle school music leaders must be cautious when dealing with sensitive issues such as sexuality, dating, family relations, drugs, and mental illness. The awful reality is that our children are exposed to adult concepts and expected to look and act in ways not normal for their developmental age. Keep this in mind as you deal with choir parents. Just as you keep your middle school parents informed about matters of schedule and activities, keep them informed about issues you discuss in choir.

Isolation and loneliness are realities when studying the habits of middle school youth. Walk through the halls of a local middle school. Notice the groups of students and how some students hang around the groups, but are not a part of the "fun." Notice students who couple with only one friend, students who are alone by choice, and students who are alone and scared. As their hormones produce unprecedented physical and mental changes, they are forced to develop social skills in an environment of heightened self-awareness, increased peer pressure, and unbridled passion. Beyond the musical and artistic values, you can partner with your youth choir parents to create a place to develop skills and awaken a heart for those who are on the social fringe of society. As you connect and involve parents in the choir, the adults model appropriate inclusion of people, affirm feelings of empathy suppressed by the harsh environment projected by the MTV crowd, explore new ideas, and help students grow in their spiritual journeys. Be careful when selecting parents to work with the young people, and understand that not all parents model proper values. In essence, your middle school choir ministry can embrace Christ's message to us found in Matthew 22, "Love the

Lord with all your heart, soul, and mind . . . love your neighbor as yourself. On these two commandments hang all the law and the prophets."

Conclusions

It is difficult to make the time to create an effective middle school youth choir ministry. The starting point of a new ministry begins with your relationship to God, call to ministry, and true beliefs. The knowledge needed to be successful with middle school youth is vast, and the personal time to make connections is a major investment. As a church musician, it is your responsibility to make informed, prayerfully considered, synergistic, and creative choices.

The thought of middle school youth ministry carries a negative connotation with many church musicians. They forget the joy that comes from working with this group of preteens and adolescent teens who are full of energy, fun-loving, and loyal. Your ministry can be filled with spontaneity, spiritual depth, artistic expression, emotional development, and social interaction on a grand scale. Activities can range from rehearsals to mystery trips with everything in-between. Middle school students are open to musical variety as they explore their newfound mental and physical abilities. They will follow your lead if you communicate vision and connect with both student and parent.

Church music ministry can no longer be conducted by marketed strategies that are neat, systematic, and well-ordered. The issues created by time, finances, spiritual health, staff relations, territorialism, competency, purpose, and philosophy (to name a few) prohibit an easy one-two-three solution or response. Each ministry situation is unique and needs the leadership of God's called artists to create effective ministries. It forces church musicians to be grounded in a ministry philosophy, committed to lifelong learning, and inspired by connection. The choice is yours.

• *John Simons is an associate professor of music at Oklahoma Baptist University and has extensive experience with middle school choirs.*

ORGANIZATIONS

Choristers Guild; YouthCue, Inc.; Cambiata Vocal Music Institute of America and Cambiata Press; American Choral Directors Association (ACDA) and the Choral Journal; Music Educators National Conference and MEJ (Music Educator's Journal); Southern Baptist Church Music Conference

REFERENCES

Jere Adams, *Leading Youth Choirs* (Nashville, TN: Convention Press, 1988).

Hilary Apfelstadt, "What Makes Children Sing Well?" *Update* 7 (1988): 1.

Emil Behnke and Lennox Browne, *The Child's Voice: Its Treatment with Regards to After Development* (London: Sampson Low, 1885).

Barbara Brinson, *Choral Music, Methods and Materials* (New York: Schirmer Books, 1996).

Don Collins, *The Cambiata Concept: A Comprehensive Philosophy and Methodology of Teaching Music to Adolescents* (Conway, AK: Cambiata Press, 1981).

————, *Teaching Choral Music*, 2d ed. (Upper Saddle River, NJ:Prentice Hall, 1999).

John Cooksey, "The Development of a Contemporary, Eclectic Theory for the Training and Cultivation of the Junior High School Male Changing Voice," *Choral Journal* 18, nos. 2, 3, 4, 5 (October 1979–January 1978).

————, *Working with the Adolescent Voice* (St. Louis: Concordia Publishing House, 1992).

Randy Edwards, *Revealing Riches and Building Lives* (St. Louis: MorningStar, 2000).

Dottie Ferrington, *The Junior High Voice* (Nashville, TN: Convention Press, 1988).

M. L. Gackle, "The Adolescent Female Voice: Characteristics of Change and Stages of Development," *Choral Journal* 31 (1991): 8.

S. Herman, *Building a Pyramid of Musicianship* (San Diego: Curtis Music Press, 1988).

John Link and Gerald Ware, *Keys to a Successful Youth Choir Ministry* (Nashville, TN: Church Street Press, 1997).

James McKinney, *The Diagnosis and Correction of Vocal Faults* (Nashville, TN: Genevox, 1994).

Richard Miller, *The Structure of Singing* (New York: Schirmer Books, 1986).

Kenneth Phillips, "Back to Basics: Teaching Children to Sing," *Choral Journal* 27 (1986): 3.

————, *Teaching Kids to Sing* (New York: Schirmer Books, 1992).

Donald Roach, *Handbook for Children's and Youth Choir Directors* (Dallas: Choristers Guild, 1987).

Frederick Swanson, "The Changing Voice: An Adventure, Not a Hazard," *Choral Journal* (March 1976).

William Vernard, *Singing: The Mechanism and the Technic* (New York:Carl Fischer, Inc., 1967).

John Yarrington, *Building the Youth Choir* (Minneapolis: Augsburg Fortress Press, 1990).

NOTES

[1] Steven Covey, *The 7 Habits of Highly Effective People* (New York: Simon and Schuster, 1989), 95.

[2] Kenneth Phillips, *Teaching Kids to Sing* (New York: Schirmer Books, 1992), 79.

[3] Don Collins, *Teaching Coral Music* (Saddle River, NJ: Prentice Hall, 1999), 135.

[4] Lynne Gackle, "The Adolescent Female Voice: Characteristics of Change and Stages of Development," *The Choral Journal* 31, no. 8 (March 1991): 24.

[5] Anthony Barresi, "The Successfuul Middle School Choral Teacher," *Music Educator's Journal* 86, no. 4 (January 2000): 23-28.

[6] Randy Edwards, *Revealing Riches and Building Lives: Youth Choral Ministry in the New Millenium* (St. Louis: Morningstar Music Publishers, 2000), 57.

Ken Avent

Youth Choir Ministry— Planting a Heart Song

Author's Note: The following paragraphs include few, if any, original ideas or insights. Instead, you will find distilled ideas of literally hundreds of youth choir directors who willingly and generously shared them with me at events sponsored by YouthCue (www.youthcue.org). Thanks to them and to Randy Edwards for the vision of YouthCue, which has encouraged and enabled so many in youth choir ministry. My volunteer work with them is a labor of love.

I got it! I finally got it! For years I had heard the concept and understood it on an intellectual level, but sitting in an airplane I experienced it and understood in a way that no intellectual exercise can begin to simulate.

Moments before, I had given my wife a last hug and boarded a plane for my first trip to Bulgaria. I was filled with a sense of foreboding and fear. I tried to reason with myself, but it seemed nothing would penetrate the gloom until, slowly but surely, the sounds of a large a cappella choir singing "The Lord Bless You and Keep You" filled my mind. Those soothing words and tunes playing on the soundtrack of my heart brought immediate relief. I worked hard to keep the choir singing as the plane taxied and took off toward the unknown of Bulgaria.

Planting a heart song—a song for the hard times—is a huge part of what youth choir is all about. On that day in March 2001, I finally understood it in a way that I never had before.

Placing that heart song requires a vibrant youth choir program that sings quality music in a quality environment. Nothing cheap or expedient will have long-lasting, beneficial effects. Scratched on the blackboard at the first youth choir seminar I attended were four words: "There Are No Shortcuts!"

Why Youth Choir? The Teen Perspective

After *you* decide to direct a youth choir, you need participants. An informal survey of young people in youth choirs will invariably generate a long list of reasons why they first came to the group. That list can easily be summarized as follows: the trip, friends, the trip, friends, singing, the trip, friends.

You get my drift! Does it matter why young people initially come to the choir? Perhaps not. If they come and find meaningful relationships, they will stay for the right reasons.

Why Youth Choir? The Adult Perspective

"All adolescents are ultimately alone in their search for identity whether at the top of a mountain or in a crowded room, flopped on their bed listening to music alone or strolling the mall in a pack. It cannot be forgotten that the self-conscious journey inevitably also occurs in a context."[1]

"A clear picture of adolescents, of even our own children, eludes us—not necessarily because they are rebelling, or avoiding or evading us. It is because we aren't there. Not just parents, but any adults."[2]

The music minister is responsible for providing a stable context for a young person's journey to self-identity. Also, parents and other caring adults are responsible for being there along the way.

Building Community

WITHIN THE GROUP

Helping young people belong to and identify with a group they find meaningful is critical to the task of adult mentors. Every get-together, whether a rehearsal, fun time, worship service, or concert, can be an opportunity to reinforce the idea of shared community. Through well-designed devotionals, prayer time, and projects such as sending cards to those in need in the church and community, the group can be led to a sense of shared purpose.

WITHIN FAMILIES

Building bridges to other members of young people's families can be accomplished in many ways. One tool with a high success rate is utilizing "love letters" on a tour or a retreat. Weeks ahead of the event, contact the parents of your young people and ask them to write their child(ren) an unconditional "love letter." Be specific that what you want is total affirmation of the child's wonderful qualities—without the qualifiers often present in communication. ("I love you, but I sure wish you would clean up your room!" is not the message you seek.) Then, at an appropriate time during the tour, distribute these letters to your youth as part of a devotional. Make sure you have plenty of "counseling time," if needed, or decompression time afterward in which these incredible experiences can be internalized.

During a different tour or retreat, surprise your youth by distributing parents' love letters early in the week. Then provide paper, pens, and stamped addressed envelopes and ask them to write a letter of response to their parents. If you plan ahead, the letters can be mailed that night and will arrive home before the young people return. Upon returning home, you will experience the joy of watching world-class reunions between youth and parents.

Note: You know your youth better than almost anyone. Please be aware of young people who are in difficult family situations. If necessary, find another caring adult to write a love letter to those teens. Make them feel as loved and important as the rest of the group.

WITHIN THE CHURCH

Involving the church congregation with the youth choir brings the entire church into the community of the group. Every service or trip is a potential connection. From worship participation to fund-raising dinners, a variety of ways is available to bring together this extended community.

One example is having adults create anonymous "goodie bags" for specific members of the group for a tour or trip. This "goodie bag" should have goodies as well as a personal note affirming that youth (by name!) for what he or she is about to do. Sign up volunteers ahead of time. Twenty minutes during a church fellowship dinner is all it takes to find "tour partners," and each year it gets easier and easier to do.

The goodie bag and note are simply a beginning! List these helpers on the tour program as "tour partners." Then, on the last week or day of the tour (to keep it fresh in the kids' minds), have each youth write a thank-you note to those who support them. I generally hand out preaddressed note cards, give kids time to write their notes, then collect and mail them so they will arrive within a day or two of our return.

Invite tour partners to the welcome-back dinner or service and do "reverse" name tags to match singers with their unknown benefactors. That brings lots of hugs and smiles and long-lasting connections.

Prayer cards also build church community. After sending out literally hundreds of prayer cards, many people in the church and community get to see a side of the youth choir they had not expected or appreciated. Not only does this dramatically affect the youth, but it also brings adults into contact with them in an unexpected and meaningful way.

WITHIN THE LARGER CHURCH AND WORLD

Hearing a youth choir sing brings joy to almost anyone. The youthful energy and simple, positive message that their very presence brings is powerful. Retirement centers, nursing homes, small churches, and other community facilities are always delighted to welcome a youth choir. By singing at these places, the youth will begin to understand how meaningful their participation is—especially with an emphasis on personal communication both before and after the service/concert. Some of the most amazing experiences occur during post-concert contact at retirement centers. Music reaches deep into the spirit, especially when sung by young people.

Building Awareness of Christian Responsibility

As the steps above are accomplished, the group begins to sense that music is simply the tool for the overall mission. Certainly, it is important that the tool be used properly and that the craftsmanship be excellent, but the goal is to spread the love of God as effectively and sincerely as possible.

In an ensemble, each member becomes aware that they are needed as part of the whole; he or she has a responsibility to the group not only to be present but also to work hard. In time, youth will realize this challenge and rise to accept it.

Building a Sense of Self-worth

Self-worth—a term used often and frequently in the negative—is, as a positive quality, so rare in young people that it is an endangered species. Certainly, their age, the season of growth, and the natural "breaking away" process are all part of that problem. Youth choirs can be a powerful force to help young people see themselves as meaningful parts of the world.

Give them a glimpse of the miracle they are. "Come O Lord, swiftly come. In my life let your will be done. Make my life a blessing so others can see, your love, your life, your miracle in me."[3]

Every rehearsal, every service, every contact is an opportunity to share your delight with how awesome youth are as miracles of life and to help them to see the value of what they are doing. Understanding the mission (bringing God's love) and understanding that young people have a unique way of communicating it are necessary concepts to learn.

"When you sense that you are indeed a messenger of God's love and know it at the root of your soul, then you will have a treasure that will never leave you."[4]

By reinforcing hard work with plenty of opportunities for fun and by thanking young people genuinely out loud, you will help them internalize your gratitude and celebrate it. Help them see how much they minister with their joy and energetic spirits. They will gradually become aware that they are ministers to everyone around them.

Building Resiliency

I began by writing about my own experience with a "heart song." Planting this song deeply is a crucial part of the youth choir experience. In his book *Revealing Riches & Building Lives,* Randy Edwards tells the story of a choir tour during which one of the members of the group found out that his father had died. The young man wrote these words to Randy: "From the moment I found out my Dad was gone, I have been hearing music in my head. It has been going like a movie soundtrack non-stop ever since. What I am hearing over and over again, without end, is the song we sing near the end of our concert, 'Cast Thy Burden Upon the Lord.' I can't tell you how comforting this has been to me."[5]

Building Musical Skills

Yes, music is important! It is the glue that binds the ministry together. Helping young people discover their musical abilities and nurture them into art is a satisfying and admirable goal. I leave it to others for the how and why of this area, but I will say that the musical skills developed in a good youth choir will remain for the rest of their lives.

Relationships

A youth choir—like so many other groups—is based upon relationships, and no relationship is more important than that of the director to the kids. A good relationship is easy to establish by following a short list of "dos."

Always be sincere and honest. We all know of stories of directors who violate this rule and how it can harm a relationship. Kids are already skeptical of adults (unfortunately with good reason). Give them the respect they deserve and they will respond to it. Be aware of what they are going through and address it. It's one thing to know about something, but kids want desperately to be heard when they talk about serious issues. I remember clearly the Sunday night after Columbine as we sat on the floor of our choir room and simply talked about feelings and fears. Nothing profound was spoken that night, but the message of love and caring was loud and clear.

Be alert to changes in mood. If something happens in the group or the attitude seems to shift significantly, stop and listen! Take time to listen, comprehend, and make changes if necessary, or be prepared to explain sincerely your position on the issue. Consistency and sincerity are crucial in such a situation.

Be available; talk and listen. It was Sunday afternoon about 4:45 P.M. I had set up everything I knew we would need for rehearsal, and I was in the sanctuary waiting for the kids to arrive. In walked a young lady with whom I had not been able to connect. She seemed to have a major chip on her shoulder and a natural reluctance to open up.

Sitting on the steps of the platform as she walked by, I asked a brilliant question like, "Hey! How are things?" "Ok, I guess," was the dejected reply. I knew I had to keep this conversation going if I was ever going to have a relationship with this young person. I pulled out all the stops and came up with this witty response: "So, what's going on at school?"

Slowly, haltingly, our conversation began to actually take form. Ultimately interrupted by the chaos of thirty kids arriving for rehearsal, our talk laid a foundation. During the course of the next three years, this shy, insecure, hurting young lady blossomed into a delightful, fun-loving, excellent singer whose very presence energized the group.

Do not ever let a conversation stop in awkward silence. The next sentence may be the breakthrough to an incredible relationship.

Listen to what teenagers want. Set parameters and give them power. Do they want to choose their own music? What is wrong with that? Let them. Select twenty-five appropriate anthems, and give them the chance to choose up to one-third of the program. You select the rest (you *are* the director). By limiting the amount they select, you will be able to balance the repertoire as well as insert a difficult and/or classical piece(s) that will require time to appreciate.

Organize officers to help with leadership and discipline in the group. Empower young people to be spiritual leaders as well and rely on them for assistance. Officers that are not used quickly learn that they are not valued.

Abide by your agreements. If you give the group (or officers) a choice, be prepared to support enthusiastically whatever they choose! That means setting the parameters so that the choices are all palatable. I have witnessed the destruction of a youth choir by a director who gave the group choices and then reneged when they chose the one he did not want.

Leadership

A youth choir will only go where the director is willing (and able) to lead it. Read that sentence again!

Teenagers will probably not tell you they don't feel challenged. They will not tell you they do not feel valued. Instead, they will gradually drift away. They will likely respond with enthusiasm or nonchalance when you ask them if they are coming next week, but if they feel unchallenged, unvalued, and uninterested, they will not show up. Leading youth choirs means challenging yourself as well as the group.

Have you ever considered doing an eight-part a cappella piece with a twelve-voice group of timid (but willing) singers? One year, my group of young people wanted *more*. They wanted a challenge. I chose a Glad arrangement of "Be Thou My Vision" for them to try. They loved it! My group of teenagers enjoyed a traditional hymn. We spent hours and hours and more grueling hours drilling parts and rhythm. Slowly, like a huge ship gathering speed, we began to make progress. I will never forget the sight and sound of those kids singing this piece by memory and a cappella at our final tour concert.

Hannah (a member of the main group) and I were drinking lemonade just before an October concert at a church we were visiting. We had little time to prepare for the concert. Hannah wanted to know if I had lost my mind and why we were doing this program. "I'm raising the bar," I told her, "to a point just within your reach." Of course, setting that bar is one of the most delicate tasks of the director. Were we perfect? Of course not. But we were there, singing and doing our best.

Randy Edwards is quick to point out that it may be music, clothing, schedule, or any number of things—but the bar needs to be raised to keep teenagers' attention and help them feel challenged to do their best.

Substance Always Wins Over Fluff!

Young people become what they ingest. Feed them quality. Examine the texts your group will be fed and make sure they are worthy. "We know deep in our hearts that what we do touches teens for time and eternity. We instinctively sense that much of life's crucial water hits the wheel during adolescence, and we know these events will have an everlasting impact upon kids."[6] In many, if not most situations in their lives, quality has taken a second place to speed and convenience.

My wife Gaile and I were sitting on a deck at our home admiring the scenery. It was quiet for a while and I began thinking back one year to the grueling task of building that deck. I had decided to do it myself because I felt incapable of explaining to someone else what we wanted, and I also wanted the experience of doing it. The commitment made, I set about planning and implementing it. I wanted the deck to be solid and well-crafted. I wanted it to look nice and last for a long time. After carefully planning it out on paper, I began from the footings up. It seemed to take forever to build, and no summer has seemed hotter than summer 2000. After literally thousands of screws and many hours of sweat and toil, I was sitting on this fine structure. It dawned on me that the satisfaction I felt was exactly what I wanted the youth in choir to feel. Having worked hard and long on something that required time and patience to put together, they would get great satisfaction from doing it well. It is wise to remember that the first step in building the deck was digging in the mud to plant good footings.

We must persevere in a society that has a case of "remote-control syndrome"; if we don't like something we can change it right away. Students spend more energy trying to change things than buckling down. They never give anything the time to decide if it is 'worth doing.'"[7] It is up to us to set the bar and gradually raise it until the choir understands that they are doing something meaningful. The idea of substance is important in the kind of challenge we offer.

Fat Folders Frame Fortes

I will admit it. I tried giving away CDs to the first teenager to arrive at choir, and then I drew a name from those of the first ten singers present and gave that person a CD. Despite my attempts, nothing worked until the day I decided on fat folders and a packed schedule.

Have you ever noticed that most successful youth choirs have regular responsibilities? I thought they had responsibilities because they were successful. Now I know they are successful because they have responsibilities.

I remember the first year I decided to have the choir learn and memorize a new piece of music every three weeks. One of the young gentlemen in the choir was sick and absent for two weeks. The following week, we met in the choir loft of a neighbor church for a dress rehearsal for the following Sunday. Without comment, I launched into a piece that we had begun two weeks earlier. I can still picture the eyes on this guy's face as we started singing the piece from memory. The more we sang, the wider the eyes got. When I remembered that he had not been to rehearsal for two weeks, I started laughing and handed him the sheet music! He told me he would never miss two in a row again.

Just Do It!

In January 1996, I attended my first YouthCue Directors' Roundtable in Dallas. Youth choir would never be the same for me. I met thirty other directors and packed more ministry ideas into my head than I thought possible. Common threads ran among all of them.

- A tour! No matter how short or small, do a choir tour. Our first tour was six concerts in two days with an overnight 300 miles away; it galvanized the group in a way I could not have imagined.
- Sectional rehearsals. Get adults or college students to lead sectionals as often as possible. It is a great way to learn music quickly.
- Have officers (or grade level representatives) and use them.
- Do good music and lots of it. Set a goal to sing on a regular schedule.
- Memorize everything. For the pieces you do not memorize, do not use the music! It was two weeks before the tour. We had been working hard on a classical piece (Handel) and struggling with it. It was not something that was in my teenagers' idiom. I was discouraged because they were not singing out and I knew they could. Because of the difficulties of the piece, I had been letting them use the music.

"Okay. Put the music down!" I said. While we may have struggled for the next couple of minutes with entrances, the sound was absolutely glorious. We made it! When I let them use the music to work on rough edges, the sound completely disappeared. It was a moment of pure excitement, and the group never performed anything while reading the music after that day.

Establish an "audition-only" group for special (and difficult) music. This gives those in the larger group a "special team" they can be proud of and relate to, and it gives some of the more talented singers a way to tackle difficult literature. It is also a great way to teach music to those who are interested in more detailed instruction.

• Connect with YouthCue. I am affiliated with YouthCue, but only because it has been such a blessing to my own life and to the lives of countless others in youth choir ministry. It is indeed the ultimate resource for youth choir directors. YouthCue offers:
  —A great web site full of information and back issues of the newsletter
  —A monthly newsletter also packed with practical and philosophical information
  —Youth choir festivals around the country
  —Recordings of great repertoire accompanied by professional orchestras at choir festivals
  —An e-mail list that shares information with hundreds of youth choir directors
  —An anthem series of accessible anthems as well as short, wonderful a cappella pieces
  —A Directors' Roundtable at which directors share and learn about youth choir ministry

Attitude

It is said that the only thing in life we can control is our attitude. The attitude we carry is also contagious. Our living the "good news" and its resultant loving attitude is the most potent force for spreading the gospel that has ever existed.

My closing is a quote from *Revealing Riches & Building Lives*:

> Why do we do what we do? The dream is to touch today's teenagers deeply with the indescribable grace of Christ. Indescribable it is, for mere words are inadequate to express it. That's why we have to sing it. Yes, touching new millennium teenagers and influencing their lives is best achieved through the medium of music. If you don't believe it, just ask MTV.
>
> Why do we do what we do? We do it because the job desperately needs to be done. When it is accomplished, even in small increments, it creates a huge wellspring of strength to all who are fortunate enough to experience it. The overflow of blessing also extends to directors and adult

leaders who associate themselves with youth choirs, those precious and priceless mentors who invest themselves in the heavenly cause of kids.

Why do we do what we do? Ask the thousands of teenagers for whom youth choir is having an enormous, positive impact upon their lives at this very moment. Ask the countless thousands who are now into adulthood and whose lives are forever enriched and fortified by the choral experiences of their youth.

Why do we do what we do? God has called. Our answer is, "Here am I, Lord, send me."[8]

• **Ken Avent** *is the CEO of YouthCue and has been an active youth choir director.*

NOTES

[1] Patricia Hersch, *A Tribe Apart—Journey into the Heart of American Adolescence* (Westminster, MD: Ballantine Publishing, 1998), 18.

[2] Ibid., 19.

[3] Pepper Choplin, *Lord, Work a Miracle* (Delware Water Gap, PA: Glorysound Publications, 1997).

[4] Ken Avent, *Celebration Singers Tour Book* (Jefferson City, TN: Ken Avent, 1998).

[5] Randy Edwards, *Revealing Riches & Building Lives—Youth Choir Ministry in the New Millennium* (St. Louis: Morningstar Music Publishers, 2000), 3.

[6] Ibid., 3-4.

[7] *A Tribe Apart,* 79.

[8] *Revealing Riches & Building Lives,* 4.

Louis Ball

Organizing the Adult Choir

Introduction

The service choir is the most important choral organization in the music ministry. For seemingly endless Sundays, this choir sings the Word to the church's largest gathering. The minister of music is judged more by the quality of the service choir than by any other aspect of his or her work. Called the sanctuary, adult, service, chapel, or chancel choir, this choir helps the minister most in leading worship.

There are two governances that operate for the service choir: (1) musical direction and (2) organizational administration. Musical decisions must remain in the domain of the music minister. Just as the fingers of a pianist's hands are subservient to the brain of the pianist, so also must musical decision remain firmly under the control of the music minister. To do otherwise is to generate discord and multiple conflicting goals for the choir.

On the other hand, the administrative organization of the service choir is best lodged in multiple hands with a cohesive structure providing direction and focus. The minister of music cannot manage this work *in absentia*. He or she must be a "hands-on" leader who leads through others.

Types of Organization

No Organization

There are degrees of organization. Of course, a service choir can function with no elected officers. While it may seem that the absence of leaders suggests a lack of organization, in actual practice, ad hoc self-appointees will handle some tasks that arise. This results in control by those with the strongest personalities.

The absence of organization appears to provide for an apparent total control by the minister of music. But this approach does not allow choir members to grow or to rotate responsibilities, and it ultimately leaves the singers high and dry when the minister of music moves to another ministry location.

A Democratic Organization

The best structure is built on democratic action. A simple constitution and bylaws lend stability and continuity. A well-organized choir supports the present minister of music and offers a stable and encouraging process to a new minister when the need arises.

Cooperation is the magic elixir; officers and members must cooperate, but more importantly, the minister of music and officers must cooperate. Proper leadership motivates members to achieve. A spirit of cooperation will produce better musical results and singers who are ready to utilize the suggestions of the minister of music in a joint musical venture.

The common denominator of Christianity in action is service. A good organization spreads service. Efficiency results along with growth and satisfaction. It seems easy for the music minister to "just do it myself." Sometimes using the organization may take longer than going ahead alone, but the long-term benefits of using elected leadership are worth the extra time required. When elected officers are slow to complete a task, the minister of music should refrain from completing the work for them. Intervening destroys the system and establishes distrust.

Shared leadership multiplies effectiveness. It also allows choir members to invest themselves in musical projects. A sense of belonging can be instilled into the largest service choir through a judicious use of officers and lay leaders.

The Organization

Begin with a written constitution and bylaws. This document should be brief, flexible, written by the members, and distributed to everyone who participates in the music ministry.

• *Step 1:* Appoint a committee to write the organizational document. Select three individuals who understand the concept of shared leadership and who have experience as leaders.

• *Step 2:* Meet with the constitutional committee. Guide the proceedings. Provide a sample skeletal constitution that may be adapted to the size and needs of your particular group. Assure brevity and adaptability in the proposed constitution. A sample basic constitution for a service choir is provided below. It may be adapted for larger or more specialized ensembles.

- *Step 3:* With the help of the constitution committee, announce that an organizational meeting of the service choir will be held at a specific time. If possible, allocate ample time for discussion, possible changes, and the vote.

- *Step 4:* Ask the constitution committee to appoint a nominating committee to present a slate of officers for the initial organization.

Following is a sample (skeletal) organizational statement for a church choir:

SAMPLE CONSTITUTION
Article One
Name
The name of this organization shall be the ( ) Choir of ( ) Church.

Article Two
Purpose
1. To lead congregational singing.
2. To provide musical performances such as anthems and service music for worship.
3. To lead in musical productions, oratorios, and dramas that celebrate the great festivals of the Christian year.

Article Three
Membership
1. Choir membership shall be open to individuals (church members) who present themselves as willing, or choir membership shall be open to individuals by audition.
2. The minister of music shall assign members to the appropriate voice sections.
3. Honorary membership may be granted to those who have retired from the service choir or who have made other contributions to the music ministry.

Article Four
Officers
The officers of the service choir shall include (1) president, (2) vice-president, (3) secretary, (4) treasurer, (5) social chairperson, and (6) librarian.

Article Five
Committees
1. Social Committee (members appointed by the president and social chair-person)
2. Executive Committee (president, vice-president, secretary, minister of music, organist)

Article Six
Business Sessions
Business may be transacted at any regular choir rehearsal. An annual business meeting shall be held in the spring to elect officers to take office the same date as regular church officers. One month prior to this meeting, the president will appoint a nominating committee to bring a slate of officers to be presented at the annual meeting.

Amendments
The constitution may be amended at any regular meeting by a majority vote provided the proposed change has been read at the previous meeting.

BYLAWS
Bylaw 1
Duties of the Officers
1. President: Preside at all business meetings of the service choir. Serve as ex-officio member of all standing and ad hoc committees.
2. Vice-president: Perform all duties of the president in his or her absence.
3. Secretary: Maintain attendance records of each member at rehearsals and services in which the service choir participates. Make a monthly report in business meeting regarding attendance. Analyze the numerical information for promotional purposes.
4. Treasurer: Receive and disburse all money for the service choir according to the instructions of the choir in business session.
5. Social Chairperson: With the social committee, lead in the scheduling of social events for the service choir.
6. Members may serve two consecutive terms as officers.
7. Section leaders for each voice part are appointed by the minister of music. They serve two functions:
   • as musical leaders of their voice part and
   • as promotional and membership leaders for their sections.

Note: Because they need to be the best musicians and singers available, it is better for the minister of music to appoint section leaders than for the nominating committee to select them.

Conclusions

The benefits of a good organization are many. Dedicated officers can help emphasize the spiritual aspect of the group. This may be the most important work of the officers for some choir members.

Social relationships are best served by the combined efforts of the social chairperson, social committee, and minister of music. For some members, the choir is the chief social organization to which they belong. For other busy people, choir may be but one of many social links to the community. At several levels, the social aspects of good choir organization are beneficial.

A good organization develops individual leadership skills that may help not only the choir but also other church groups. Reading about leadership may not be as important as the experience of one term in office.

The concept of shared leadership facilitates and underscores the principle of the priesthood of the believer. While there is a close fit between shared leadership and democratic church governance, there is also correlation in churches that have an ecclesiastical hierarchy. Those who are skilled pass their talents on to those less experienced. A well-defined method of organizing the service choir is worth every effort.

• *Louis Ball is the retired Dean of the Division of Fine Arts at Carson-Newman College, and the recently retired secretary-treasurer of the Southern Baptist Church Music Conference. He has served in numerous full- and part-time church music positions.*

Tracy Wilson

The Church Handbell Program

Why Bells?

As I began to think about this topic I first had to ask myself why. Why have a handbell ministry in your church and as a part of the total music ministry? The cost can be quite high for the small- to medium-sized church. Are we justified in spending $5,000-$10,000 for this program? How does having a handbell program spiritually edify people? I support handbell ministries, but it is important to consider the reasons for them.

Over the years, the outstanding educational value of a handbell program has been demonstrated in the arena of music education, especially when used with children. My church has three bell choirs for children in grades three, four, five, and six (fifth and sixth graders are together). We also have a youth bell choir and an adult bell choir. When children join the handbell ministry, directors have a wonderful opportunity to teach the elements of rhythm through bell music. Note reading is learned as children ring bells and find notes. Therefore, there is a strong opportunity to teach elements of music as ringing techniques are learned. I have been amazed over the years to see children progress in their music reading skills. It is not unusual to have piano teachers and school music teachers complement the handbell ministry in relation to music reading. The handbell ringer who is also studying piano or a band instrument benefits greatly from ringing. Playing in the bell choir reinforces many concepts members learn in band and piano practice. There is also the opportunity to teach music expression markings. The ringers should learn certain markings like piano, forte, repeat signs, etc. Learning to ring expressively is crucial to making music. These expression techniques should be addressed in a handbell choir.

Secondly, a handbell ministry is a wonderful opportunity for spiritual education. As ringers play hymns and other music, they are exposed to great spiritual truths. The director can encourage ringers in their knowledge of Scripture. As the ringers perform in services, they learn about worship and what it means to lead in worship. The handbell director should take time in rehearsal to discuss what it means to lead in worship. We never ring to entertain or to receive applause. We ring only to praise Jesus for his love and grace. God is the object of our worship through ringing.

Finally, there is an outstanding fellowship value for all age groups in the handbell ministry. Many adults will join a bell choir who would never join a vocal ensemble. Many adults have instrumental backgrounds and seek a place to use that skill. Children's bell choirs offer great fellowship for children as they rehearse during the week. The groups at our church meet after school and always include time for a snack. This is great for social interaction for the children. During rehearsal, ringers also enjoy the camaraderie of mastering the skill of ringing and working as a team. Do not underestimate the power of bell choirs for your church.

How to Begin

For churches with no bell choirs, several steps heighten interest. Perhaps the church has bells but no active groups. What do you do?

The first step for a church with no handbells is to determine the interest or need for handbells. The best way to test the congregation's appetite is to invite a guest bell choir to your church to lead in worship. The rule of thumb is to make sure they are a high-quality group. This does not mean they have to be the best choir in the region. They simply need to be a group that will leave a positive impression on the congregation about handbells and their role in worship. A churchwide survey is an excellent way to determine interest in a bell ministry. Include questions that will help the director identify potential ringers, such as previous musical background in instrumental groups or vocal groups. Ask about potential rehearsal times. Discuss the idea of a handbell ministry with the church leadership, such as the church council, the pastor, and the music committee. Pray for God's leadership. It may be that the timing for this ministry is not right. Always strive to follow God's leadership. Explore the cost of handbells and the necessary equipment. At this stage, the person who spearheads this ministry needs to have an idea about the amount of money required.

The second step in beginning the bell ministry is to consider the physical needs for bell choirs. The choir will want basic equipment like handbells, tables, music, folders, foam, foam covers, and music stands. Visit an area church with a bell program and note the supplies they have for bells. Learn the name of their source for music and supplies. Jeffers Handbell Supply, one of many handbell suppliers, will provide a free catalog that includes equipment prices (1-800-JHS-BELL or www.HandbellWorld.com).[1] There are primarily two brands of bells used by churches in the southeastern United States—Malmark and Shulmerich. Both are high-quality handbells that are easy to find on the web. Not only will the church need to purchase bells and equipment, but there must also be a place for the bell choirs to rehearse. It is preferable to have an area where the director can leave the tables set up between rehearsals. Many churches have a choir room or music suite where this is possible. Some churches will not have this luxury. Work through the proper committee or board to locate and receive permission to utilize an area for rehearsal. If it is a room shared with other groups, the tables may have to be put away after each rehearsal. Do not despair; many groups begin this way. Have the adults, youth, and older children who ring help store the bells and equipment after each rehearsal. It is not fun, but it is worth the effort.

The director must decide on the ages of the choir(s). How many choirs are needed? Should adults and teenagers be in the same group? In my experience, this is a difficult combination. Teens are still children in many ways. Adults tend to get frustrated quickly with the way teenagers rehearse and conduct themselves. There is nothing wrong with teenagers being teenagers. However, most adults want to be in a bell choir with other adults. I would mix these two groups if that were the only way two or three teens would have the chance to ring. The best course of action is a bell choir of similar ages and maturity levels. Some ministers of music begin a bell choir with a group of children and then try to keep them together as a group through high school. They may not all be in the same grade or of the same age, but they start together and stay together. The director should address these issues before offering an invitation to join a bell choir. The level of music reading is an issue. A good reader will be frustrated in a choir of nonreaders. Is the intent to establish a bell choir of music readers who will ring difficult music from the beginning, or is this a group of beginners?

The next step in starting the church handbell program is to secure approval from the proper committee or body in the church and raise money for the purchase of the bells and equipment. An appropriate amount of interest in the program should already be established. The person who presents the dream of a bell ministry to the church or to the appropriate committee should gather information and anticipate questions. How much do the bells and equipment cost? Where would the choir meet? Who would be involved? How would the bells be used? Think through these questions and have answers.

Raising money is frequently a difficult issue. After approval has been given to start this ministry, the appropriate body in the church should decide how the money is to be secured. Will it come from the church budget and general offerings? Will there be a memorial fund established? Would one or perhaps several people underwrite the effort? Will a special offering be taken? Be prepared and know the costs involved. Have an informational handout ready to present.

When approval has been gained and money is being or has been raised, it is time to enlist ringers and/or directors. The minister of music may direct all the bell choirs. Or, there may be a need for several different directors. If so, the minister of music should enlist them with the approval of the appropriate committee(s). The minister of music should have considerable input in the enlisting of lay leaders. The director needs to be someone who reads music and has experience with bells. The person should be caring, compassionate, patient, and have a love for music and people and an understanding of the purpose of the bell choir program.

As ringers are enlisted, keep in mind the kind of choir the director is trying to establish. Is this a choir that will attempt difficult music soon? If so, experienced ringers will be needed or at least people who read music fairly well. Is this a choir for beginning ringers or for children? If the desire is to start a choir on a come one, come all basis, make an appeal in the church newsletter or bulletin. Be specific about when the choir will start, where it will meet, and how long rehearsals will last. Be specific about needs for music reading level, age, and maybe even gender if a ladies' or men's choir is the goal. Some enlistment may need to be done face-to-face. If the goal is an experienced choir, the director may want to invite specific ringers, hand-picking that choir. This would probably be in a large church situation. Care would need to be taken not to offend someone and to be tactful in approaching ringers. Be specific about the goals of the group.

First Rehearsals

When you begin first rehearsals of any group, it is important to focus on the basics. Begin with how to hold the bell. The bell is held between the thumb and fingers with the fingers snug against the collar of the bell. The last three fingers are kept loose to help with ringing.

The second basic is the ringing stroke. The bell should be held in an upright position, and as the ringer rings the bell should be dipped as if imaginary water were in the bell and would be spilt. There is some discussion as to how the ringing stroke should be executed. I usually teach a stroke as a

D shape, never ringing above the shoulders. Cynthia Dobrinski, a well-known handbell instructor, rings in a "painting" stroke. The main point is to teach all the ringers to do the same stroke.

The third basic of handbell ringing is how to dampen or stop the vibration of the bell. Many ringers and choirs ignore this basic of bell ringing. There is nothing more distracting than notes being held too long or too short. This is a vital part of bell ringing and should be taught from the beginning. Use quarter note, half note, and whole note patterns as teaching material. The director should teach beginning ringers to dampen at the proper time and in the proper way. The edge of the bell rim should be touched just above the breastbone near the collarbone, but not on the collarbone.

Another basic to teach the beginning ringer is the parts of the handbell and how to recognize when the bell needs adjusting. There are several small parts to the bell that loosen when a person rings it. The ringer needs only basic knowledge of those parts. The most common problem is the clapper loosening while ringing. It is held in place by a small screw that can be tightened when needed. There are quick adjusting clappers available for some handbells that allow clappers to be moved quickly to a soft or medium setting. Another common problem is a stiff or loose clapper in the ringing stroke. If it is too loose, the ringer will experience a back ring or double ring. If is too stiff, a shake can be difficult to execute. There are two small nuts on each side of the clapper that are adjustable and affect the setting. Spend time acquainting the ringer with these parts. The director should be able to disassemble and assemble a bell. The bells the church purchased should come with a diagram of how this is done. If that is missing, contact the company sales representative for assistance.

Begin rehearsals with easy rhythmic patterns. The first experience should be ringing one hand at a time. There are a few books available for the purpose of teaching beginning rhythms, or you may write your own. Use whole notes, half notes, and quarter notes only. Rehearse ringing the bells at the same time. Do not let the ringers get in the habit of ringing off the beat and not together. Drill this technique until they are proficient. It is wise to focus on reading easy rhythms in the beginning and delay note reading for a few weeks. Beginning groups are still trying to ring properly and learn rhythms.

After a few rehearsals, begin to teach ringing two bells at a time. There are exercises available to help teach the skills associated with ringing two bells. Some of those skills are damping one bell when striking the other bell, table damping, and switching bells between hands. An excellent resource from Harold Flammer Music is "Coordination Conundrums" by Valerie

Stephenson.[2] This resource offers drills that will help ringers master important skills. There are many books that can be of aid, or you may write some
of your own exercises.

Before you begin the first piece of music, make the following decisions
for your choir: how you will assign the bells, and whether the ringers will
keep these particular bells throughout the year or will move to other bells.
Assign the bells based on the number of bells versus the number of ringers.
Each ringer should ring two diatonic bells and the associated chromatics
such as B4 and C4. These two bells also involve the ringing of Bb4 and C#4.
Seven or eight ringers can handle two octaves, eleven ringers can handle
three octaves, and fourteen ringers can ring four octaves with the bass ringer
ringing three bells. Consider the abilities of the ringers. Some ringers can
play four-in-hand and cover four bells and their chromatics, which is an
advanced skill. With beginning groups, there may be a ringer or two who
need only to ring one bell for a while. Plan ahead for these issues. If the
ringers are allowed to move, they will not be able to ring difficult music
unless they are advanced music readers. I find it best for a ringer to stay with
the same bells for at least one year.

Maintaining a Handbell Ministry

Long-range planning is a must for a successful handbell ministry. Bell choirs
need to play regularly and set goals. Schedule your group to play in worship
as soon as possible. This gives everyone something to work toward and
quickly focuses rehearsals.

Begin from the outset to instill a high level of commitment in the group.
Encourage adult ringers to secure a substitute if they will be absent.
Distribute a substitute list. Help them understand that their consistency at
rehearsals makes or breaks the musical group. It is difficult to develop skills if
there is no consistency in rehearsing. It is difficult for a group to develop the
ability to ring together if they are not all present at rehearsals. Remind the
group frequently about the necessity of being present.

Plan as soon as possible to take adult and youth bell choirs to a handbell
festival. Festivals are wonderful ways to challenge your group and hear other
bell choirs who are learning. At the first festival, you may want to observe
only. Most festivals use several mass ringing pieces. Your beginning group
can participate in the mass ringing pieces only and learn a great deal.

One issue that arises as you develop a bell choir is "to mark or not to
mark your notes." Many beginners want to mark their bells, and it is a helpful aid for the person who does not read music. Children can begin in this

way. However, by the time they are in middle school, ringers should not rely on this crutch. Coloring or marking notes leads to rhythm reading only. This is an issue that the director must consider individually. Many adults want to color or mark their notes. Will you allow this? It is a crutch, but is this the only way that a certain adult will participate? This can be argued both ways and is a personal decision for the director to make.

• *Tracy Wilson* *is the minister of music at First Baptist Church in Dandridge, Tennessee, and the director of a graded handbell program.*

RESOURCES

Unlike fifteen years ago, there are many resources available today to the bell director. Use the internet to search the word *handbell*, and numerous sites will appear. There is an excellent organization available for the director called the American Guild of English Handbell Ringers, Inc.[3] This organization provides a quarterly newsletter with information about festivals and many other resources. One excellent publication from that company is an informational booklet titled "Handbell Notation and Difficulty Level System."[4] This booklet standardizes the notation system for handbell music and the rating system for each piece of music. Other helpful resources for beginning groups include the following:

Gerald P. Armstrong, *Let the Children Ring!* (Nashville, TN: Broadman Press, 1986).

Martha Lynn Thompson and Frances Callahan, *Begin to Ring* (Carol Stream, IL: Agape/ Hope Publishing, 1986), #1242 for 2 octaves; #1243 for 3 octaves <www.hopepublishing.com>.

The Handbell Curriculum (Dayton, OH: Lorenz Corporation, 1986) <www.lorenz.com>. This is an excellent series of teaching books for beginners. Titles include "Rhythm Skills," "Standard Hymns," and "Favorite Hymns."

The above list is useful primarily for beginning groups. For more advanced ringers, there are many publishing companies with an abundance of music available for all sizes of groups. Happy ringing!

NOTES

[1] Jeffers Handbell Supply, PO Box 1728, Irmo SC 29603-1728.

[2] Valerie Stephenson, "Coordination Conundrums," Harold Flammer Music, HP5373.

[3] AGEHR Inc., 1055 E Centerville Station Rd., Dayton OH 45459-5503.

[4] Ibid.

Jeff Cranfill

Building a Church Instrumental Ministry

Psalm 150 instructs us to praise God with instruments. The primary purpose of a church instrumental program is to bring glory to God. While there are many facets to such a program, prayer is the key to motivation, attendance, personnel, finance, and growth. Ephesians 3:20-21 says, "God is able to do immeasurably more than all we ask or imagine." Prayer gives us God's power, presence, provision, and perspective. When God establishes an instrumental ministry in a church, the necessary ingredients will be present.

An orchestra adds a new dimension to a worship service—whether playing by itself, with the choir, or accompanying congregational singing. Instrumental music is most effective in worship when the music brings to mind the text of the song or provides a background suitable for Scripture meditation. It is a great blessing to instrumentalists to minister with their gifts and skills.

The Called Servant or Volunteer Player

Instrumentalists are trained to be performers. Instruments are purchased and hours are spent in practice to be ready to perform. In a church ministry, players need to be taught that they are not there to perform, but to minister. More than volunteers, they are there because God wants them there, and they are to obey God's call by being present and prepared.

In a worship service, God is the audience. The music is not for the entertainment of the congregation. The instrumentalists are not to play for the approval of the people. Their performance is for the worship and praise of God!

Starting a Program

Make sure the pastor and other church leaders are in full support of beginning an instrumental group. A pastor's support in and out of the pulpit is effective and vital.

Here are ideas for beginning an instrumental program:

- Pray that God would bring the players necessary, as well as meet the scheduling and budget needs.
- Select a date to begin rehearsals and a date for the group to play in a service. A goal for a certain worship service is important to get players motivated.
- Advertise church-wide and in the community for interested players.
- Have players call in advance to register to help determine what music can be played.
- Select, purchase, and distribute music before the first rehearsal. Select music that glorifies God, ministers to your congregation, and suits your group.
- Love and encourage the players in rehearsals; make them feel welcome.
- In the service, the orchestra can play solo pieces (preludes, offertories, and postludes) or accompany congregational singing. There are several instrumental hymnals available.
- Have an all-church orchestra. Invite everyone who plays or has played an instrument in the past to come for a one-time event on a Sunday afternoon. Make the music available ahead of time for those who want to practice. Rehearse together that afternoon, have dinner together, then play during the evening service.

As the orchestra or instrumental ensemble plays in services, it becomes easier to invite other players to join. While ministering to the church, an orchestra is also a great outreach tool that attracts instrumentalists to the church.

A church orchestra is unique in the musical world and differs from group to group. Most often it consists of a wind ensemble, a rhythm section, and hopefully strings. Fortunately, there is a wealth of music available to accommodate unusual instrumentations.

Instrumentation

Publishers produce music on two or more levels. The most advanced level (usually known as grade three or four) is written for a standard minimum instrumentation: two flutes; oboe (optional); two clarinets; two horns—doubled by alto saxophones; three trumpets; two trombones—doubled by baritones, tenor saxophones, bass trombone, or tuba; bass—string bass, electric bass, or keyboard bass; drum set, timpani, mallets, and other percussion; piano; organ (usually); harp (optional); guitar—most arrangements include rhythm chord charts; two violins; viola; cello—doubled by bassoon and bass clarinet; synthesizer string reduction. String parts are usually optional and can be covered by a synthesizer playing the string reduction part. There is also music available for smaller groups with limited instrumentation, from duets and trios to small orchestras.

The organ can be a great addition to an orchestra. Rather than replacing and perhaps alienating a faithful organist, have the orchestra and the organist work together. There is room for both in a worship service.

Recruiting Ideas

The recruiting process must be continual. God will bring new people in and move other people out. Perhaps the most effective recruiting occurs when the orchestra ministers effectively and sounds good. Success breeds success to a degree.

- Have orchestra socials—parties, games, meals.
- Have a friend day. Invite an instrumentalist friend to rehearsal.
- Use word of mouth. Personal invitations are the most effective. Have the players make contacts and invite people from their Sunday school department, neighborhood, school, or work.
- Announce needs for players in church publications: "The orchestra would like to add a flute player . . . ," etc.
- Bring in an outside group to do a concert. Perhaps combine the groups.
- Bring in well-known solo performers to play or sing with the orchestra.
- Ask someone to join the orchestra for a particular event (Christmas musical, etc.).
- Have the orchestra play concerts in the church and community. Occasionally, guest conductors can be used for variety and another perspective.

- Visit high school band and orchestra rehearsals. Help the director with sectionals, etc., or be an extra pair of ears. Ask the school director to invite good players to your program. A church orchestra can effectively build sight-reading, knowledge of key signatures, tone, and confidence.
- Hire players on occasion. They might be willing to come back on their own or help spread the word to other players in the community about the group.

Preparation

"Sing to the LORD a new song; play skillfully with shouts of joy" (Ps 33:3). Playing well is biblical. Whenever the orchestra ministers in services or concerts, the music should sound good. Those who claim the name and power of Christ, in this case church musicians, should be well prepared.

Preparation for Rehearsal

The players must enjoy their conductor, enjoy the rehearsal, and know that they are accomplishing something. They are giving their time to God, not to the director, and the director must be prepared to make maximum use of it.

Include a pencil in every folder. Encourage players to mark accidentals, counting problems, repeats, and other things that could be missed. This method serves as a great reminder and time saver, since most church orchestras meet only once or twice a week.

Plan the order of pieces and note the ebb and flow that occurs in most rehearsals. Do warm-ups, familiar pieces, and easier sight-reading early in the rehearsal. In the middle of the rehearsal, it is time for hard work, details, and the music for Sunday. The director should schedule sight-reading and challenging projects late in the rehearsal. Always end with something your musicians like and perform well.

The players need all of the music in their folders in advance. Check each piece to assure everyone has a part and that all parts are legible. Edit difficult parts prior to rehearsal. It is helpful to have a librarian distribute music before rehearsals, find parts during rehearsals, and collect music after services.

Prepare and distribute rehearsal notes that include rehearsal order, announcements, information, prayer requests, schedule/calendar, and sign-out slips for planned absences.

The director must be musically prepared. Study the scores carefully. Look for tempo markings and changes, keys and key changes; note which instruments have the melody or solos; discover which instruments have accompaniment/harmony; anticipate spots that need rehearsing—difficult or unusual passages or lines that will probably need specific attention; and find unusual chords/harmonies, often including accidentals.

Conducting Instrumentalists

Effective and efficient conducting saves valuable time in rehearsal. The conductor's gestures and facial expressions should convey to the players the tempo, style, and dynamic of the piece being played. Players must look at the conductor every few measures and at key moments (tempo changes, entrances, etc.). It is helpful for the director to evaluate conducting techniques from time to time to ensure that the players are getting what they need. Videotaping rehearsals or services sometimes helps.

- Use a baton. Instrumentalists, for the most part, look at the conductor less often than singers; they are reading their parts. A baton gives focus to the beat pattern and helps players see the beat more clearly when they look up.
- Rather than counting off or giving one "measure for nothing," give a good preparatory beat. The preparatory beat should clearly convey the tempo of the piece or section, dynamic, and style.
- Give a clear downbeat in each measure.
- Cue players' entrances after long rests.
- Conduct from the full score whenever possible. This helps you see the big picture of the piece and know what all musicians are doing at any given time.
- Conduct the entire piece—including introductions and endings.
- Conduct during sustains if there are moving or rhythmical parts.

In Rehearsal

Keep the rehearsal pace brisk and interesting. Time off task usually prompts inattention by the players. Let the orchestra play.

- Keep directions and instructions to a minimum, except for devotions.
- Do not stop often to work out problems.
- Use a brief warm-up. Give attention to tone, intonation, balance, blend, key signatures, or following the conductor.
- Give directions once. Repeating instructions too often trains players not to pay attention to the director's words.

- Give specific and detailed instructions when correcting a player ("watch the key signature; do not let that note go flat; that rhythm should be played this way").
- Use appropriate, good-natured humor consistent with your personality.
- Count measures together when starting in the middle of a piece ("Count with me measures before letter B—1, 2, 3, 4, 5, 6, 7—let us begin there.")
- Some talking in the group is okay. Rehearsal is one of the few times some of your musicians see each other! If socializing gets out of hand, lovingly reel them back in.

When performance time arrives, convince the players they are ready to play. Church instrumentalists must develop confidence with little rehearsal time; the players need to know the director is satisfied with their preparation.

Musical Results

Instrumentalists who play with a good tone are much more likely to play in tune. Players need to play with the best sound they can produce. To improve the tone, play long tones with a slight crescendo at the end, and use range scales and range-building exercises. As performers' upper limits rise, their tone and control improve.

Tuning

Tune the group after the warm-up. Tuning is the process of having players conform to a standard pitch. Tune to the piano or a tuner. The strings tune first on "A." Next, the woodwinds tune on "A" or "B♭." Then the brass on "B♭." Tuning is not an event; it is a process. Intonation changes as players warm up, experience fatigue, and encounter room temperature changes. Players must constantly listen and adjust their instruments. They need to know when they are out of tune. If they cannot tell whether they are sharp or flat, use trial and error. If they lower their pitch and the problem worsens, raise the pitch, and vice-versa.

Players and the director need to know the pitch tendencies of their instruments. Know how range, dynamic, endurance, and temperature affect each instrument and how to compensate for changes.

Ensemble Sound

When the director hears something that does not sound right, the problem must be determined and the best solution found. Having a section or several sections play can make musical problems easier to find and fix. Generally, there are three ways to address musical problems:

(1) Correct the problem. Sing it to them, rehearse sections and/or individuals before or after rehearsal, take a slower tempo, then speed up.

(2) The problem will get better on its own. Run through it again. The better the players are, the more likely musical problems will correct themselves.

(3) The problem is not going to get better. The player is not capable of playing the part. Edit the part in advance if possible, or omit it. Do not embarrass the player. Sometimes, a poorly written part is to blame.

If the group sounds ragged, listen for:

• *wrong notes*—key signature mistakes are common causes of wrong notes.
• *blend*—players must listen to themselves and those around them. If the players cannot hear those around them, the players are too loud or are not playing strongly enough.
• *style*—everyone should play the same length of quarter and eighth notes (staccato, legato, etc.).
• *balance*—make sure the melody is predominant in the texture. Then make sure all other parts are present and slightly less prominent than the melody.

If a group plays well, they are more willing to continue playing well. Strive to make music on each piece rather than simply playing notes. God created music to affect our emotions. When the correct notes are played with good tone, in proper rhythm, dynamic, blend, and balance, the sound can be wonderful!

Inform the orchestra members how their ministry touches hearts in the congregation, including the director's heart. As people comment on how the orchestra is a blessing to them, share it with the players. A church orchestra can be a great blessing to both a congregation and the participants. Remind them of the unique privilege of instrumental ministry.

Attendance

If the orchestra performs frequently, the players are more likely to come to rehearsals. When they have a specific goal—service, concert, recording project, etc.—players feel a greater sense of urgency to be present at rehearsal.

Players need to be reminded they are called to play skillfully (Ps 33:3), which involves preparation—both individually and corporately.

Have a flexible, well-published attendance policy. There are times when players cannot be at rehearsal, especially when it is trumped by a higher priority (family needs, etc.). Players need to know they are free to fulfill God-given priorities in their lives. One such policy might look like this:

(1) Be here. When you are not present, there is no one to take your place.
(2) If you must be absent, contact the director in advance.

The people need teaching and reminding—all in love! When individuals miss rehearsal or a service, a note or phone call from the director and orchestra members letting them know they were missed is helpful.

A church orchestra generally sounds better with more players present. If certain parts are missing, some pieces will not sound complete, and some are not useable. Set goals for orchestra attendance and make the goals known to the group. Groups usually move toward goals that are set.

Fellowships (in homes, parties, meals, picnics, socials, games, attending concerts) can help build group morale. Rehearsal can be ended early periodically and refreshments served to celebrate birthdays or holidays, or simply to thank players for being there. It is more enjoyable to rehearse and minister with friends than with strangers.

Directors must be sensitive to the people's time. Rehearsals should start and end on time. People are more willing to give time when the steward of that time is trustworthy.

The church director needs to understand that in ministry situations with unpaid players, attendance will be low on occasion. Lectures and scolding are most often counterproductive and inappropriate. Continue to pray, teach, and encourage without becoming angry or discouraged.

Equipment

When instruments or equipment are needed, there is an opportunity to take requests to the Lord. God responds to faith and prayers.

Compose a list of needs at budget request time. Remember to consider instruments and equipment, including purchase and repair; music—orchestra, ensembles, solos, educational/training materials; occasional hired musicians; clinician for orchestra concert or retreat; computer/software; training/conferences; office supply needs; printing/postage; food for socials, officer meetings, etc.; transportation to off-site performances; and awards.

When purchasing instruments and equipment, always look for quality. Good used instruments are often a better deal than lesser quality new instruments. Local music companies are sometimes willing to give better deals to a church. Establish and build relationships with local music stores. It is helpful at times to borrow from and loan music and equipment to local schools. The Internet also offers resources worth consideration.

Keep orchestra instruments and equipment in good repair. The orchestra rehearsal area/service seating area should be neat and uncluttered. This is consistent with an organized, quality program.

Library

Use a number system for the music library. Enter all pieces in a database computer program and keep current printouts. Music folders are best stored in portable folder storage cabinets or racks. Keep originals of all music and distribute only copies. This is consistent with church music copyright laws and helps ensure all parts will be available to all titles.

Remove music from the players' folders after it has been played. Music is easier to find in uncluttered folders. When players wish to take music home to practice, make copies for them so that the players will always have the music they need in rehearsals and services.

Church/Staff Relations

Whether a member of church staff or a volunteer the orchestral director can be most effective if these ideas are followed:

- Work to make your minister of music and pastor successful (Prov 27:18).
- Communicate. The director must not assume that others know and understand all that is involved in effective instrumental ministry.
- Make proposals only when you have all necessary information. Appeal humbly. Help your minister of music/pastor see what you see—why your proposal is necessary.
- Have a good reputation. Be a team player.
- Check the church calendar when scheduling events and place orchestra events on the calendar. Also check local school and community calendars.
- Be involved and interested in other areas of church life.
- Consider the effects of orchestra events on other church ministries when planning.

Orchestra Seating/Setup

The orchestra setup is often dictated by where the orchestra sits for rehearsals and services. The following guidelines will help determine the best setup for any room:

- All players need to see the conductor.
- Players need to hear each other. If they are seated too far apart, use monitors to help them hear.
- The rhythm section (piano, bass, drums, guitar) needs to be as close together as possible.
- Set the instruments in their family groups (consider doublings): rhythm/percussion, brass, woodwinds, strings.
- Place louder instruments and instruments lower in pitch in back, softer/higher instruments in front.

Symphony orchestras and concert bands balance their sounds by sheer numbers; they have enough strings and woodwinds to balance the number of brass players. Church orchestras often do not have enough strings and woodwinds to balance the brass section. Amplifying strings and woodwinds and careful instrument placement can help create a pleasing balance within the orchestra.

Balancing Orchestra and Choir Sound

Combining church choirs and orchestras can add a powerful dimension to worship. In smaller churches or with smaller choirs, the orchestra can be overpowering. The following are common-sense techniques for balancing the orchestra with the choir: (1) The text is most important in a choral work. When the choir is singing, players must listen for the singers. If the message cannot be heard, then the orchestra must play softer until it comes through. (2) When singing with an orchestra, the choir must sing out. The orchestra can play loudly on introductions and transitions and then play more quietly while the choir sings. The words must be heard.

Pray for the right attitudes of everyone involved. Singers and players are to minister *together* to the glory of God. Instrumentalists need to be lovingly and kindly informed when they are playing too loudly for the situation. Consider this from the players' perspective; they need to know the director appreciates their efforts and skills. Players also need to know they are part of the larger picture of worship and that the message must come through.

Sound Strategies

• Use sound absorbers/reflectors—sonex, plexiglass, carpet, etc.
• Keep uncovered brass away from the choir microphones.
• Rewrite or omit impossible-to-balance parts.
• Use fewer players during hard-to-balance passages.

Do not expect the impossible. If the orchestra parts are written full, high, and strong, or the choir is small, balance may not be possible. Sometimes the choir and orchestra need to do separate pieces. With prayer, planning, and persistence, most of the balance problems can be solved.

Spiritual Growth and Ministry

Musical preparation must take a backseat to spiritual development. The most important activity for any director is to pray for the players. Set aside time to pray for each one by name. Get to know their spouses' and children's names, and keep track of events and issues in their lives when you learn about them. Let the people know you are praying for them. Modeling love for God and passion for ministry sets a spiritual growth standard for the people in the group. The players need to hear what God is doing in the director's life. Spiritual zeal is contagious!

The director must be spiritually prepared for each rehearsal and performance. The players need to be bathed in prayer for the needs in their lives and their daily walk with the Lord. Pray also for the needs of the orchestra ministry. Prayer is the antidote for worry; it gives God's power, presence, provision, and perspective. The director, the individual players, and the group as a whole should continually lift the ministry in prayer.

Devotional Time

Include a brief and concise devotional time during rehearsal. Present a spiritual "nugget" through Scripture and the texts of the songs and hymns being rehearsed. It is easy for instrumentalists to get caught up in the notes and neglect the message of the songs.

Spend time with orchestra members outside of church. Visit players in their homes, in the hospital, and in funeral homes when there is a death in the family. The orchestra director is the shepherd of the orchestra.

Motivation

Sacrifices of time, skill, effort, and money are given by orchestra members. The players need constant reminders that their service is important. Christians are to do their work with all their hearts, as service to God (Col 3:23-24). King David said he would not offer to the Lord that which costs him nothing (1 Chr 21:24).

• *Jeff Cranfill serves as a music minister in Loganville, Georgia, and has made significant contributions to the instrumental church music repertory.*

Chris Alford

Hiring and Working with an Orchestra

It is a joy to welcome outside, professional musicians to your church, and there are a number of places and times where it is appropriate and even ideal to do so. At its best, using outside musicians can be a wonderful way to enhance worship and beautifully compliment the hard work of choirs and ensembles. While the topic of this chapter is limited to the use of outside professional musicians, keep in mind that meaningfully and appropriately using avocational musicians in the church is a wonderful ministry and an important goal of any music minister. Identifying those people and finding the right way to use them is an important topic worthy of a separate chapter.

Why Use an Orchestra?

Before hiring professional musicians, think about why you want to do so. Hiring musicians means spending money, and spending money can be a problematic subject in church. Apart from the issue of resources, it is always a good idea to have a clear understanding of why you want to hire professional musicians for a ministry program. Ponder these issues and develop a sound rationale for using professional musicians in the church.

There is strong theological support for employing musicians in worship. I recommend Marva J. Dawn's book, *Reaching Out without Dumbing Down: A Theology of Worship for the Turn-of-the-Century Culture* (Grand Rapids: Eerdmans, 1995). In chapter 1, Dawn makes a convincing case for churches to rethink how and where they spend "their" money in relation to worship. Most churches pay significant sums for facilities or outside professional help (i.e., legal or architectural) and think little of it. All too often, worship gets overlooked. Worship is the purpose of the church; a significant amount of the church's resources should be invested in this priority.

I believe using professional musicians in worship aids and enhances the experience of those who worship. I am also convinced that the way to build a musically sound ministry, and especially a musically sound choir, is to sing challenging repertoire that may require hiring professional singers. Experience in ministry has taught me that the works that mean the most to the choir tend to be the more challenging ones. There is nothing quite so musically and theologically satisfying as significant repertoire, those wonderful choral monuments that have stood the test of time, as well as the plethora of newer gems. What a terrific time to be a music minister!

This chapter focuses on using a chamber orchestra, which is a tremendous challenge to the choir and director. It stretches our skills and takes us to new musical places to which we might not have ventured otherwise. Using professional musicians, especially as an accompaniment to the choir, is a treat the choir deserves. After months of rehearsal for a Christmas program, having a professional ensemble accompany the choir is a delightful way to reward them, perhaps exposing them to a new level of musicianship, greatly increasing the level of overall performance and enhancing worship at the same time. Have you ever worshiped when the opposite took place? I have. I recall attending a service where a choir's hard work and dedication, not to mention worship, was horribly ruined by the use of student players who were inadvertently placed in a difficult spot and not up to the task.

Professional accompaniment is a wonderful way to enhance performances; unfortunately, the opposite is often true when nonprofessionals are used.

Questions About Using an Orchestra

How many musicians do I need? The quick answer is not as many as you might think. It is useful to consider the type of worship service in which they will play.

The published cantata, which sometimes is the easiest program to tackle, often calls for more instruments than are necessary for a successful performance. (Though I generally dislike the use of the terms "program" and "performance" when talking about worship services, the nature of the topic lends itself to using them in this case. One of my highest goals as minister of music is to focus on worship with God as the audience.) Cantatas are written by composers, arrangers, and orchestrators who have the luxury of creating with far fewer limitations than most music ministers. Few publishers seem to consider the equipment, budgetary, or personnel restraints most of us encounter. Also frustrating is that the works are recorded by professional instrumentalists and singers in ideal studio settings with a gorgeous result that is nearly unattainable by the average church. Even if the music minister hires all of the professional musicians indicated by the score, the choir may be swallowed up in sound, fighting a losing battle with gaggles of winds and brass and exotic percussion instruments.

How do I solve some of these problems? The first step is the knowledge that you do not have to hire or fill all positions for which the score calls (apart from the strings). If you study the score, you will undoubtedly notice that many of the instrumental parts are copied, or "doubled," by other instruments, especially brass parts. For example, third or fourth trumpet parts are often doubled by other brass instruments. If not, they are rarely crucial to the overall sound of the piece. Orchestrations are primarily an elaborate, musical "fleshing out" of the piano or organ part. Many instruments can be omitted without harming the sound.

Step two is to consider the result of, for example, eliminating all the parts called for except pairs of winds and brass. I have consistently used only single winds and pairs of French horns and trumpets for years with great results. You may have to do creative rewriting, but the results will be saved space, budget, and a more controllable ensemble. The correct way of designating this arrangement (single winds and pairs of horns and trumpets) is: 1-1-1-1; 2-2-0-0. The numbers correspond to what is called "score order" of the instruments, a standard listing that is used in the orchestra world and refers to this order: flute, oboe, clarinet, bassoon; horn, trumpet, trombone, tuba.

Regarding percussion: A good player will often be able to cover adequately both the timpani and the auxiliary percussion parts. Sometimes, though, two players are necessary. Similar to the decision to hire extra brass or wind players, a balance must be struck between how busy and/or necessary the part is versus the expense of hiring.

Many ministers have little experience with orchestras and tend to make the most mistakes in the use of stringed instruments. The string section of the orchestra needs to be full and rich. Strings sound better and even play better when there are more of them. One general, but accurate, rule of thumb is to think of the string section much as you would the choir. The top strings (first and second violins) are like the soprano section. Currently, string scores for some church music only provide for a single violin part, but the standard is two, and even single string parts often divide into two parts. The violas are much like the alto section of the choir. The cellos roughly correspond to the tenor and baritone range of the choir. The bass violin, like the bass singers in the choir, round out the roster.

Do not make the mistake of having too few strings—and too few of the inner voices. A rough guide for string numbers, based upon the orchestra size I normally use for special services, is four first violins, three second violins (generally slightly fewer seconds than firsts), three violas, two cellos, and one bass (though bass parts sometimes double cellos, the low register makes a big difference in overall sound). The correct way ("score order") of designating this arrangement is 4-3-3-2-1.

What about designing my own program? I mentioned earlier that in some ways the published musical or cantata is the easiest program to tackle. The program that features many separate works is more difficult. Examining the parts, looking for places to eliminate instruments that double others unnecessarily, and making sure a particular instrumentalist has enough to do throughout the program to justify the hiring expense are time-consuming.

Constructing these types of programs is more problematic, but I think they are also rewarding. Many music ministers think they can put together a better program than the published cantata. The first challenge is to locate quality literature. There is a veritable mountain of music available, and most of it will not be appropriate for your uses. How do you narrow the choices? You could attend music-reading sessions and workshops, but I believe the best way to find good music is to talk to colleagues. Ask music ministry friends to tell you about their favorites. Use networks and associations to help you find great music.

When you find a collection of works you would like to use, think through questions such as these before you add them to the program:

(1) Does the piece meaningfully add to the overall theme of the service?
(2) Is there a good balance between slower and faster selections?
(3) Is there a pleasant balance of styles?
(4) Do the chosen works and the order of presentation move listeners toward a conclusion to the worship service?
(5) Do the pieces generally feature the same orchestral instrumentation? Are hired musicians being used responsibly?
(6) Is the overall length of the program appropriate?

Should I hire the musicians myself or seek help in doing so? Many music ministers engage the help of an outside person—often a local professional musician—to make contacts and hire the personnel needed. This person is called a "contractor" and is generally paid twice the normal rate for this service. This is the preferable choice because the minister makes one call with the details and the contractor does the rest. The contractor takes the list of instrumental needs, records dates and times for rehearsals, contacts the musicians, and makes all the arrangements. However, you might prefer to do some or all of this yourself, especially when you know individual players and want to make specific personnel decisions.

The key for making your presentation a success is early planning. For a special Christmas program, dates and times for rehearsals and performances "in-house" are verified first, carefully placing all events on the church calendar with approval from appropriate people, committees, etc. Musicians should be hired by September. Musicians' calendars fill quickly and prompt action yields the best players. Confirmation of rehearsal and performance dates/times, fees, and any other details about repertoire, special instruments, etc., must be negotiated.

Most professional musicians are accustomed to playing church "gigs" and will have an established fee. Learn the present rate from other musicians or from your contractor. If you have difficulty, contact the local American Federation of Musicians (AFM) office (the union for professional musicians) or the local symphony orchestra. Organists often know many local instrumentalists because of their frequent association with them for weddings and funerals.

Musicians are accustomed to working in segments or blocks of time called "services." This is not to be confused with a church service. Most professional musicians understand that a service is a segment of time, usually two and a half hours, spent in rehearsal or performance. There is generally no difference between the service rate for a rehearsal and a performance.

Musicians are customarily hired for at least one rehearsal and also for the number of performances anticipated. For a program that will be performed only once, musicians would be enlisted for two services (i.e., a Saturday morning rehearsal and a Sunday evening performance). Occasionally musicians work in extended services (i.e., a three-hour service), where the rate is slightly more than for the two-and-a-half-hour service. It is technically possible to have a rehearsal and a performance in the same three-hour service, but definitely not recommended.

The local symphony orchestra and (or) the AFM office usually drive the details about services and rates. Most importantly, the hired musicians are professionals who deserve a fair and appropriate wage in keeping with other engagements in the community.

When musicians have been contracted, the church is obligated to pay them even if the concert is cancelled or dramatically modified. A verbal contract with them requires that the church make good on your promise to pay them. Musicians reserve time on their busy calendars and will lose income if you do not make good on your promise. Sadly, I have heard of churches earning a poor reputation with the professional musicians in town because of the music minister's lack of planning.

Preparation for Rehearsal

The most common mistake made in preparation for the dress rehearsal has to do with the music itself. Most ministers do not adequately prepare the actual sheet music that will be given to the musicians.

Here are a few suggestions to avoiding pitfalls:

• Make sure that each player has the correct number of musical selections and that each piece has the correct number of pages.

• Most published cantatas have separate books, neatly arranged, for each musician. If you put together your own program, provide "tacet" sheets for musicians who might not play during one or two of the pieces. A tacet sheet is a blank piece of paper with the title of the work, the word "Tacet" centered in the middle, and the instrument's part obviously indicated. This is a courtesy so the musician will not spend time trying to find a part to a piece he/she does not play.

• Provide a folder, clearly marked with the instrument's name, for each musician.

• When an orchestral part has extended measures of rest, it is helpful to write cues for the musicians. This might be a word or two of the text the choir sings or perhaps a note about an important entrance or solo from one of the other instruments. This helps musicians keep track of long sets of rests and helps them feel more confident about their own entrances. A pencil should be used when the orchestral part or score is marked.

• Musicians appreciate having the music placed in the folder in rehearsal order.

• If a work is in a particularly difficult key or features difficult key changes, key signatures should be marked as helpful reminders.

• Bring extra parts and scores to the rehearsal and organize them so that a specific work/part can be quickly located if the need arises.

It is helpful and courteous to correspond with musicians in advance of the rehearsal, even if a contractor made arrangements for you. Secure the names and addresses of the musicians and send them a helpful, short reminder approximately ten days before the service. Include the following information:

- Place(s), date(s), and time(s) for rehearsal and performance
- Map/directions to the rehearsal location
- Note describing performance attire
- Description of the repertoire (offer to send music to musicians in advance as needed)
- Sincere welcome to the church

Sometimes music ministers less familiar with orchestral instruments worry about where to place the musicians. Narrow or cramped spaces in many churches make this task difficult. The accompanying diagram gives a generally accepted overview of the typical orchestral placement of instruments, including the choir. Eventually you will want to take the advice of the musicians themselves, who will have good ideas about the best location for their chairs and stands and will be happy to suggest them.

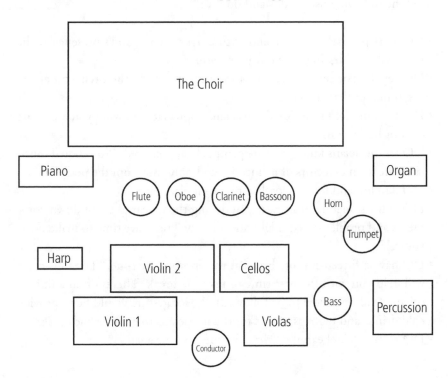

Some Handy Tips

1. Pairs of strings share music stands. Others do not.
2. Harp/bass usually bring their own seats.
3. Save extra stands for the percussion section.
4. Have name cards on the stands for the musicians.

There is no substitute for preparation, especially for the leader! Often the music minister wears "multiple hats" and tends to get pulled in many different directions, especially when the performance is a large production with special lighting or drama.

During dress rehearsal with the orchestra, the minister's most important priority is the music due to the expense of the orchestra. Wasting time is poor stewardship of resources. The most important element of personal preparation is understanding the score. The director must know and be familiar with the music.

The Rehearsal

The musicians have arrived; the choir is warmed up and ready. I have developed the following list of "dos and don'ts":

- DO start precisely on time and with prayer. Invite God's presence at the rehearsal and blessings on your preparation.
- DO let the concertmaster (the first violinist) tune the orchestra at the beginning of the rehearsal.
- DO be humble. Professional musicians appreciate knowing you are aware of your limitations.
- DO let musicians know they are genuinely appreciated. Professional musicians are keen detectors of insincerity and nonsense from the podium.
- DO develop and follow closely a rehearsal plan.
- DO enlist someone to sit near you during the rehearsal to jot down comments and problems that might arise. You will not have time to make notes yourself.
- DO have a fifteen-minute break at the appropriate time. (The musicians will help you with the best time to take the break. This is often a union-oriented rule expected to be followed). A nice gesture would be to provide cold drinks and perhaps snacks for the musicians to enjoy at the break.
- DO restart the rehearsal on time (be sure to tune again).

- DO save five or ten minutes at the end of the rehearsal for low-priority items.
- DO remind musicians and the choir about performance details (where to park, when the performance begins, where and when to gather, where to store instrument cases, and when and where the orchestra will receive their paychecks, etc.). Do this at the beginning and end of the rehearsal.
- DO end the rehearsal precisely on time.

- DON'T be remotely condescending or mean-spirited, and never browbeat the musicians or the choir. Musicians will not want to return to the church, the choir will lose faith in you, and you will do a disservice to your calling and God's kingdom if you behave unkindly.
- DON'T allow talking and time wasting in the choir. Prepare them ahead of time for the need to pay close attention during the dress rehearsal.
- DON'T "rehearse" the orchestra first, then repeat it again later with the choir. This is a waste of time, annoys the musicians, and bores the choir. Often, large portions of a work do not need a second look, or places that you originally thought might not need much attention require a second or third rehearsal. The choir will need as much time as possible with the orchestra, especially getting used to the sound. Start the rehearsal from the beginning with both choir and orchestra.
- DON'T waste dress rehearsal time on long portions of dramatic dialogue, for lighting/special effects cues, or especially for things that do not involve the orchestra (i.e., a cappella or other non-orchestrated pieces).
- DON'T try to use technical terms when you are unsure what they mean or how to pronounce them. Generally avoid excessive talking. Be yourself.
- DON'T be afraid to tell the orchestra to play more softly if needed. Good musicians appreciate musical leadership.
- DON'T ask the musicians to stay "five more minutes." Use rehearsal time wisely and economically.

To baton or not to baton . . . that is the question. It is not necessary to use a baton when conducting an orchestra. Several conducting giants of the orchestral world do not use one (Kurt Masur, for example). Some ministers may feel the orchestral musicians expect the conductor to use a baton, but this is not so. Most importantly, the conductor should express clearly and communicate with ease what is desired in the music. Most ministers of music do not generally use a baton and have not had much training in its effective use. Pulling out the gilt rosewood baton once or twice a year may make a difficult situation even more problematic. If the conductor is more clearly expressive with the baton than without, and is more comfortable using it, then a baton should be used; otherwise, abstain.

What the musicians expect may surprise you! Musicians are like you and me: they appreciate good music, attention to detail, and not having their time wasted. They also appreciate a conductor who understands the music and leads an effective rehearsal. They particularly appreciate being treated with kindness and sincerity.

Perhaps like me, you have played many instrumental "gigs," including church jobs too numerous to count. Church jobs are some of the more difficult, according to my musician friends. I am sad to report that some Christians can be terribly unkind, disrespectful, and cheap. Treat musicians with genuine respect, honor them for the gifts they bring to the church, and respect their lifelong commitment to music. If you do, they will work extra hard to support what you are trying to accomplish. Show Christ to them with your attitude and behavior.

Does the order in which you rehearse the music matter? Yes! There is an art to putting together the rehearsal order, and if close attention is given, a better, smoother rehearsal will result. Rehearsals can get stressful and time seems to fly by! It is important to develop a rehearsal plan ahead of time. Consider these helpful ideas as you plan:

(1) Arrange your rehearsal order beginning with the piece that requires the most players and ending with the piece that requires the fewest. This will allow you to dismiss players as their work is finished and avoid their sitting around with nothing to do for long periods of time.

(2) When rehearsing a program with many separate selections, budget ten to fifteen minutes for each work.

(3) Keep a "running tab" on how much rehearsal time has expired when writing down the order and the names of the pieces to rehearse.

(4) Allow tuning time at the beginning of rehearsal and after the break.

(5) Include the time and length of the break in the rehearsal plan.

(6) Allow time at the end for announcements, etc.

(7) Make sure the rehearsal plan actually makes time for each of the selections where orchestra is indicated. Compare a printed program for the performance with the rehearsal plan to avoid omissions.

Part 5: The Performance.

Remember the following tips for the performance:

(1) Keep a cool head. At most performances, something invariably goes wrong. If you anticipate minor mishaps, they will be less stressful when they occur. Even after planning, rehearsing, and working hard, odd things will happen: power failures, crying children, late musicians, broken strings, knocked-over music stands. These are part of performing!

(2) Help the musicians through the performance. This is especially important if your program includes many different sections or pieces. The musicians will appreciate knowing what tune is next, or perhaps a reminder of the tempo. They will respond well if they know you have the program under control.

(3) Pay your musicians promptly. This will be one of the most important things you do at the performance. I recommend that you place the musician's check inside a personalized envelope, perhaps with a note of thanks, and have it waiting on the music stand when the musician arrives.

• ***Chris Alford*** *is the Minister of Music of Smithwood Baptist Church in Knoxville, Tennessee, and was formerly an executive with the Knoxville Symphony Orchestra.*

Lewis Oswalt

Budgeting for the Music Ministry

Budgeting is an administrative skill in which the music minister typically has little training or experience. Thankfully, one need not be an accountant or bookkeeper to develop the requisite expertise.

Most churches organize and prioritize expenditures through the implementation of an annual budget in order to match projected expenses as closely as possible with anticipated income. Budgeting for a calendar year is the most common approach, though it is not uncommon for a church to use different dates for its fiscal year, especially if it observes a "church year" that does not correspond with the calendar year. Money matters are important in every church, just as they are to individuals. As such, those who serve in staff positions should take them seriously. Careful adherence to church fiscal policy and diligent oversight of budgeted funds are imperatives for every church musician.

A budget may be viewed in the narrowest sense merely as a form of control over financial resources. While this aspect of budgeting cannot be denied, it is also true that a budget is a means to insure that a ministry area will be able to implement plans made by the leadership. This view, which sees the budget as a means to implement a planned program to enhance spiritual growth and further the purposes of the church, puts both the concept and the process of budget planning in a more positive light.

Therefore, detailed and thorough calendar planning must precede budget preparation if the music ministry is to reap the maximum benefit. Once plans are made, the budget is constructed in such a way as to provide necessary funding. A budget proposal that reflects the vision of the leaders in the music area, as well as careful planning by those leaders, will be relatively easy to present and to defend before the committee preparing the church budget. Likewise, a vague and poorly organized budget will be viewed negatively.

This method of viewing and constructing the proposed budget allows for "zero-based" budgeting, which is the method employed by many congregations. This concept requires that each annual budget be newly constructed, without consideration for previous allocations. Thus, each proposed expenditure is examined critically and objectively on its merits without assuming its inclusion in the final draft. Though there will be some budget categories that are always present, zero-based budgeting does not allow for merely adjusting figures from the previous year's allocations. For that reason, it is always helpful to consult the budget for the current year while preparing for the year ahead.

Though the music minister is normally the person charged with submitting the budget proposal, it is important to include key leaders in the process. This allows the minister of music to assume the role of *compiler* rather than bearing full responsibility for every detail. An informed and involved music committee or music council can be of great assistance in this process. Ideally, these people will have been involved in the detailed planning mentioned above and will be mature leaders able to view the "big picture" rather than taking a narrow view due to specific interests. The inclusion of these key laypeople may be a significant factor in securing approval of the budget as proposed.

The budget proposal is in most instances submitted to a committee charged with preparation of the overall church budget. The committee is normally composed of a cross-section of the church membership. This committee will accept and consider requests from the various ministries of the congregation, each of which is convinced of the need for adequate funding of its program for the upcoming year. While it should not be said that the various ministry areas are in competition with one another, it is often true that the total amounts requested exceed anticipated income, requiring the committee to make difficult decisions. This fact should serve to emphasize the importance of careful preparation and presentation of the music budget proposal.

The proposal as submitted to the committee should be detailed in every respect, including the number of copies of music to be ordered, the cost per copy, the charge per piano for tuning, etc. Organization is also an important element; major headings should be clearly defined and easy for committee members to comprehend. A detailed proposal with good organization will in many cases answer most questions that arise. This detail may, however, be less desirable for the general church membership. Therefore, it may be prudent to prepare a one-page version, listing major divisions and amounts, to give to the congregation when the entire budget is presented for adoption.

The organization of the budget request may be dictated by church policy, but it will more likely be at the discretion of music ministry leaders. The best approach is to identify major headings. Possibilities might include:

I. Music Literature
II. Leadership Training
III. Promotion
IV. Postage/Supplies
V. Equipment
VI. Maintenance
VII. Salaries

Another approach is to subdivide the budget according to age-group ministries, with headings similar to the following:

I. Adult Choirs/Ensembles
II. Youth Choirs/Ensembles
III. Children's Choirs
IV. Instrumental Groups
V. Postage/Supplies
VI. Salaries

Ongoing expenditures that should be listed in the annual budget may include any or all of the following: cleaning of choir robes, tuning/maintaining instruments, literature for all groups/ensembles, office supplies/printing expense/postage, honoraria for guests/substitutes, instruments for children's choirs, awards, banquets/fellowships, retreats/tours, new equipment.

Other specific needs in the music ministry will become obvious in the course of daily activities throughout the year. With this in mind, it is a good idea to maintain a file in which such needs can be noted before they are forgotten or overlooked. This file then becomes an important part of the budget planning process for the next year.

It is never appropriate to "pad" budget figures as a means of obtaining surplus funds or to request large sums for "miscellaneous" spending. Such an approach will inevitably lead to the conclusion that the entire budget request does not reflect the careful planning necessary for the music ministry to garner the monetary support needed for its programs.

When preparing a budget for the first time in a new place of service, the music minister should be aware of a number of factors. A list of such factors would include but not be limited to the following:

(1) Does the church use dated (monthly, quarterly, etc.) literature? If so, are funds for music literature included as a line item in the literature area of the overall church budget, or are they charged to the music budget?

(2) Does the church provide funds for use of vans and/or buses through a transportation budget, or are the various ministries charged for their use?

(3) Are salaries (music minister, accompanist, secretary, etc.) part of the music budget or included within a larger personnel budget?

(4) Are office supplies, postage, long-distance telephone service, and school-supply items used by children's choirs provided for elsewhere or are they funded through the music budget?

It is generally better if most or all of these items are included in the music budget, if for no other reason than that it gives the church membership a clearer indication of the total amount required to fund the music ministry. Regardless, it is worth the time to examine the existing church budget closely enough to determine whether there are places where music ministry expenditures are "hidden."

Once the church adopts the budget, it is imperative that the music ministry stay within allocated funds. In fact, the importance of this basic tenet of administration cannot be overstated. A music minister who consistently disregards spending limitations may encounter significant resistance if church leaders discover this behavior. While it may be impossible to foresee all circumstances and necessary expenditures, careful planning and consistent adherence to approved policies will minimize the need to request authorization for additional amounts during the fiscal year. Likewise, church leaders who have noted a music minister's care in approaching the budget will be more likely to grant such requests when they become necessary.

To insure that the budget is not overspent, the music minister should keep an accurate record of expenditures rather than being totally dependent upon a financial secretary or treasurer. While this may appear at the outset to be difficult and time-consuming, the abundance of low-cost accounting programs currently available for personal computers makes this relatively easy regardless of one's previous bookkeeping experience. Accounts can be readily set up that only require entering expenses in the proper categories.

As a practical matter in keeping with accepted business practices, a church may require the submission of a numbered purchase order for all purchases. This helps in bookkeeping and insures that the proper budget area is charged for each purchase. The music minister should carefully adhere to this practice where required.

In some instances, churches require authorization in advance for all purchases beyond a certain amount ($200, $500, etc.), even when the expenditure is included in the budget. This is usually implemented to insure that the church does not overextend itself by committing large sums of money within a short period of time. Likewise, the church may allow each ministry area to spend only one-twelfth of its budget allocation in any given month (or one-fourth per quarter). This approach requires the music minister to anticipate expenditures that must be approved in advance and to submit requests in a timely fashion.

Rarely will a music ministry be able to purchase all needed items in a given budget year. One possible solution to this problem, especially as it relates to the purchase of more expensive items, is to budget a percentage of the total amount needed for several years. The funds are then placed in a separate account until the total amount has been accumulated, at which time the purchase may be made. Such an approach may be helpful when anticipating the purchase of robes, keyboard instruments, or sound equipment, for example.

Living with budgets is a fact of life for every church musician; living within the limitations they impose is an important model of good stewardship and the proper way to administer a vital and effective music ministry.

• *Lewis Oswalt is an Associate Professor of Music at Mississippi College, where he teaches church music courses. He frequently serves as an interim minister of music.*

Louis Ball

Buying and Storing Choral Music and Music Equipment

Introduction

The largest tangible purchase for a full program of church music is the collection of choral music. The second largest purchase might be the musical equipment, particularly that which supports a fully graded choir program. Proper storage of these purchases and organization of resources are imperative.

Acquiring the Music

Acquiring music involves several steps: finding music, choosing the best, and locating sources. We are experiencing a time when there is too much music. Publishers flood the market with new releases much as the television industry floods the cables with too many choices. The problem is to choose the best.

Before the best can be chosen, there must be a standard by which to judge. The "best" is always related to categories. There is no one piece that is the "best of show." We want the best renaissance, baroque, classic, twelve-tone, aleatoric, contemporary Christian (etc.) selection for one particular Sunday that our choir can sing. That narrows the choices considerably. It is like choosing the best horse in a race of three-year-olds as opposed to the fastest mammal on earth. There are apples and oranges in music. Therefore, the minister of music must have multiple standards to select the best. Music ministers with no standards are dupes waiting for the first advertising blitz.

Text Above All

A *sine qua non* (without which, nothing) is the text. It has been said that the person who chooses the music of a church chooses the theology. The theology is carried in the text.

The first check is a reading of the text. If the text is not biblical, then it might be a restatement of biblical passages or ideas. If the text is not a paraphrase of the Bible, then it at least must conform to the general teachings of the local church. There must not be a spurious message in the text, no matter how beautiful the music sounds.

Finding the Music

• *Festivals*—Take advantage of the results of another person's search. Music for festivals usually involves the combined work of several people, all of whom are chosen for the task because of their experience. Music chosen for state festivals is usually (not always) of better quality than a random choice from a publisher's annual output.

• *American Choral Directors Association (ACDA)*—The annual conventions of this organization (national alternating with regional) can be counted on as a parade of first-quality repertoire. Such a convention not only offers all types of the finest choral literature, but it also includes a presentation of many selections by premier choirs of all ages and makeup from around the country and the world. Attend with notebook in hand. While the difficulty level of pieces on the program may be mostly beyond that of your church choir, ACDA will nevertheless help every attendee to develop standards of tone, precision, repertoire, and interpretation.

• *College and high school choral concerts*—These groups, like those on ACDA programs, usually sing selections that are carefully screened.

• *Contest and adjudication lists*—Choral selections that have been included on required lists for adjudication for all age groups usually represent the best thinking of a group or committee of specialists. Ask your local music education organization to furnish you copies of such lists. Remember that some so-called children's pieces are acceptable for adults to sing.

• *Direct mail club*—Every music minister is flooded with invitations to join music publishers' mail clubs. Members receive copies of new publications and recordings for review. Each publisher tends to specialize in one style of music, although the annual lists may branch out into related types of literature. Ministers of music who use this method of finding music should ascertain the publishers that specialize in the type of music desired and then subscribe to only two or three publishers.

- *Summer assemblies*—Denominational summer camps often use outstanding choral clinicians who bring excellent music. Attend rehearsals, take notes, and not only listen to the music itself, but also observe how it is taught.

- *Reading sessions*—Publishers and music jobbers conduct reading sessions to sell music. These sessions are a combination of entertainment, hype, recreation, and salesmanship. It is possible to find good choices at reading sessions. The minister of music should note that there are considerable differences among reading sessions, depending on the typical style of music published.

Choosing the Best

The full resources of one's musicianship must be utilized when making decisions about repertoire. The right music can make a poor choir sound better. The opposite is also true. Weak selections will still be weak even if sung by a good choir.

- *Text first*—Remember these three judgments: (1) biblical, (2) biblical paraphrase, (3) acceptable theology. Finally, one should look for beautiful poetry. The best theology should not be sullied by doggerel.

- *Learning the music*—One cannot buy intelligently what one does not know. Begin with the music in hand. Keyboardists should play the music through, both accompaniment and parts (as possible). This is the quickest way of familiarization. Vocalists should sing enough parts to evaluate voice leading and should play enough harmony to ascertain the harmonic vocabulary.

- *Listening*—Listening to a recording is the least beneficial method of getting acquainted with new compositions. Sample recordings tend to fix interpretation and vocal sound in place before the conductor has a chance to analyze the music.

- *Rate the music*—As you examine sample copies of choral selections, assign a rating to each. Place the rating on the top right corner of the cover. My rating system is as follows:

Rating	Explanation
0	Discard—too bad to pass on!
1	Doubtful—give it away.
2	Keep and file. It is worth another look.
3	Buy if you have the money. File.

Don't labor over the ratings. Learn to rate quickly. Store samples. Keep sample copies of highly rated (2 and 3) choral selections. File by title or category. A vertical file drawer can file several hundred choral samples. Purchase alphabetical dividers and file at least once a month. Throw away bad music. Don't let it fall into someone else's hands.

Sources

More sources are available than many churches can afford. A rule of thumb is that the more services offered (samples, sorting, etc.), the higher the price. Full-service jobbers may send packages of music selected according to your particular needs; for example, you may request sample copies of three-part women's ensemble, easy, for Advent. Discount jobbers may do little more than sell at a reduction. Speed of delivery is often related to a higher price.

Each choral selection may be assigned a category according to the text such as Christmas or Easter. Another classification is that of the performing group, for example, adult, youth, children, etc. A database must be flexible enough to sort the collection so that a properly organized database can bring an immediate list from your library of, for example, SSA works for Advent or SATB selections for Palm Sunday.

Every individual set of choral music must be given a shelf number that can indicate its storage location, include its voice type, and also assign it to one or more topical categories. Here is an example:

Prefix Letter	Voice Type
A	Adult, generally SATB but could include SAB, unison, or SSAATTBB
Y	Youth, may be SATB, SAB, SA, etc.
C	Children, usually unison or treble
E	Ensemble, such as contemporary ensemble
V	Volume, a collection of anthems. Each anthem should have a separate entry for each title indicating topical category.
M	Major works (oratorio, cantata, music dramas, etc.)

Besides indicating the appropriate choir for each choral piece, one should assign it to the appropriate category. One might use the Christian Year as a beginning: Advent, Christmas Eve, Christmas Day, Epiphany, Lent, Palm Sunday, Holy Week, Tenebrae, Good Friday, Easter, Pentecost, Ascension. Expand the year by secular days such as Independence Day (patriotic), Memorial Day, Labor Day, Thanksgiving, etc. It is entirely possible that one text might be appropriate for more than one type of service. If so, make an entry for each category.

Following is another list of topics that embrace most church choral selections: adoration, Bible, Christmas, church, comfort, commitment, communion, confession, cross, dedication, discipleship, Easter, faith, grace, heaven, Holy Spirit, home, Jesus, love, missions, patriotic, peace, praise, praise and worship, prayer, redemption, service music, spirituals, thanksgiving, worship.

One should also create a set of abbreviations used consistently in the instrument category to make computer searches possible: br = brass, cong = congregation, fl = flute, gui = guitar, hb = handbells, hrn = horn, inst = instruments, pc = percussion, rec = recorder, str = strings, syn = synthesizer, tpt = trumpet, trb = trombone, tmp = tympany, vln = violin, ww = woodwinds.

Cataloging Choral Music

Since this is not a chapter about using the computer, you will need to know how to build and use a database. Learning these tasks will help you organize your resources. Some church recordkeeping systems have included in their software the ability to make a database of choral music. Your first step is to learn about this system. If you must furnish your own, find an easy program, learn it, and stick to it.

Each choral selection receives two types of cataloging. The first is the shelf number. The second is the topic or category for which the selection is appropriate. Other designations are fields in the database, for instance, the choral group for which the purchase is intended, and special additional parts such as added instruments or handbells.

The shelf number can be followed by the choral group code. Following is a sample card that illustrates all the categories in the database. You may set up the database according to your own preferences.

Example of Category Cards

Title _____ **Text** _____

Composer _____ **Arranger** _____

Publisher _____ **Publ. No.** _____

Price _____ **Difficulty** _____ **Voicing** _____

Category _____ **Group** _____

Solos _____ **Instruments** _____

Shelf Number _____ **No. of Copies** _____

A completed card might look like this:

Title Create in Me _____ **Text** Pslam 51 _____

Composer Smith _____ **Arranger** Jones _____

Publisher Brown _____ **Publ. No.** 1202 _____

Price $1.25 _____ **Difficulty** Easy _____ **Voicing** SATB ____

Category Confession _____ **Group** Adult _____

Solos None _____ **Instruments** Fl _____

Shelf Number 113A _____ **No. of Copies** 65 _____

The Database

Each bit of information on the card above requires one "field" in the database record. Therefore, each can be sorted so that all selections on "confession" or other fields can be listed together. This may not seem important when one is beginning a collection, but when the collection numbers in the hundreds, it is imperative.

Proper cataloging is also important for the minister of music who comes to a church with an existing library. One cannot simply look through a library or look at rows of boxes and comprehend the collection.

The shelf number allows the collection to be placed on shelves consecutively without regard to choral organization or number of copies. In other words, file by number. This library is not a browsing library. It is a storage library. One will use the computer for browsing. Two possible exceptions are volumes and major works. If you are purchasing large numbers of copies, it may be best to devise a separate shelf number for each of these types and shelve them individually.

Every copy of music needs to be stamped with the name of the church, city, shelf number, and copy number. This allows music to be filed quickly. It also allows a choir member to receive the same copy each time the anthem is sung. Inventory is easy with this type of system. The librarian arranges the set in numerical order. Missing copies can be traced to individual choir members for retrieval. This is a sample individual copy of music stamp:

First Baptist Church
Harmonyville, USA
Shelf No. 215A
Copy No. 14

Storing Choral Music

Multiple choral copies can be stored in unused spaces, but the ideal is to have storage and work space together. There is a lot of activity involved in preparing copies for storage. There is also space required for the distribution and collection of copies every Sunday. The ideal shelf space is one that utilizes floor to ceiling with shelves constructed just far enough apart to hold sets of music. The best storage method is the most expensive. Storage boxes with tops are the preferred protective storage items. The shelf number and title can be fixed on the front for quick identification. Catalogs of library supplies, especially those specialized for music, offer sources for good storage boxes. Other types of boxes are of lighter board construction but are not as easy to use.

Vertical envelopes are the least efficient if shelf storage is used. Vertical file cabinets are fine for the storage of choral music, provided the collection is not large. It is easy to see how much space is needed. Measure the thickness of an average set of music and multiply by the number of sets to find the number of inches needed. It is easy to fill up a file drawer.

Distributing and Collecting Choral Music

The best and most efficient method of distributing and collecting choral music is the tilting shelf system. With this system, each choir member is assigned a numbered space on a shelf that angles at about forty-five degrees with a shelf edge on the bottom to keep the music from sliding off. It is much like a series of long music stands divided vertically into space for every choir member. Several layers of shelves can be arranged on one wall, much like a large bookcase but with tilting shelves.

Music can be distributed by the librarian, who, walking along the shelves, places the copies numerically on each section. The choir member then places the newly distributed music in his or her own folder, which is also lying on the shelf. The shelf edge needs to be deep enough to hold the folder and probably a hymnal. Music is collected after a performance by the choir members, who place the used anthem on top of their folders for pickup by the music librarian. Another method of distribution is by slots for each choir member above their robe storage. Vertical slots are not efficient for distribution or pickup, but they do provide each choir member personal storage space.

Storing Music Equipment

Music equipment for the graded choirs tends to be a problem as the choir program grows and more instruments are needed. The solution is a room with shelving, perhaps eighteen inches to two feet wide. This is required for autoharps, xylophones, and Orff instruments. Posters that are useful from year to year can be stored in cases intended for house plans. Always think big when planning for storage space. There is never enough and our tendency is to provide only enough for the present.

Summary

Stewardship is paramount when one is storing materials bought with contributions given for the work of the church. Good storage with meticulous documentation insures the avoidance of duplicate purchases or lost items. Care taken at the outset is worth all the effort expended. Besides, generations after you will rise up and call you blessed for beginning storage in such an organized manner.

• *Louis Ball is the retired Dean of the Division of Fine Arts at Carson-Newman College, and the recently retired Secretary Treasurer of the Southern Baptist Church Music Conference. He has served in numerous full and part-time church music positions.*

Donald Clark Measels

A Final Word: Situation Preparation

There are several situations the minister of music can expect to arise during the course of ministry. The predictability of certain circumstances allows the music minister to think about possible reactions in advance. To react on the spur of the moment and without due consideration often results in ill-advised words and actions, thereby causing more difficulties in the future. With appropriate forethought, it might be possible to do no further harm and, hopefully, to help the people involved.

The following case studies depict possible scenarios and indicate critical factors to consider. They are intended to be hypothetical and only for contemplation; I provide no solutions. It may be helpful to remember Benjamin Franklin's maxim that we view the end before we begin. Many actions almost never have positive outcomes. The minister of music should catalog as many problematic behavior patterns as possible and be on guard not to act them out.

A minister should consider the following factors, among others:

- What is the situation?
- Are the sources of information credible and dispassionate?
- Who is immediately involved and what are their reactions?
- Who will be injured?
- Who are the extended members of the church and community who are touched?
- How does this affect the music ministry and/or the church?
- Is immediate action required?
- What can a minister do to help? (Seek many options. If possible, find a dispassionate mentor with whom to discuss the problem.)
- If action needs to be taken, who should take it?
- What is the most redemptive resolution? What are the other possibilities, including the worst conceivable outcome? What plans do you have for those eventualities?

Each problematic situation is unique and affects a minister's response. A minister of the gospel must be fair and honest and try to help people grow toward living Christlike lives. When dealing with problems, our most important choice is how to react. However, even fairness and honesty can come at a price. It is prudent to count the cost of any planned response in advance and to be prepared for the worst-case scenario.

Case Studies

(1) We recently renovated our church and installed a four-manual organ—a celebrated instrument whose presentation deserved a special event. The problem: with the new massive instrument, the organist now plays too loudly! I receive weekly complaints from the congregation about the volume during the choir numbers, orchestra numbers, and congregational singing. "I can't hear myself sing," says one person. I have politely talked to our organist, but he denies that it is too loud. People write notes to him; he discounts them. What do I do now?

(2) I discovered that during choir, one of my children's choir assistants yelled at three sixth grade students in front of many people. She cursed them, physically put her hands on them, and generally caused a scene. We've had problems with this lady before in other areas with children (verbal assaults, etc.) and know we are dealing with a variety of liability as well as credibility issues for our church. She sings in the adult choir and her husband is a main worker in developing a successful ministry in the church. What am I to do?

(3) The choir is preparing for the Christmas cantata. A singer who has not been in the choir for several months asked for a copy of the sheet music and a tape of the cantata. She intended to learn the cantata at home, come to the dress rehearsal, and sing with the choir. What should I say to her?

(4) Recently during practice for the Christmas musical, I was approached by a choir member who said he was leaving the choir because I had not given him the solo he wanted. He thought I should remove the person I had chosen for the role and place him in that position.

(5) A high school senior who has not been attending church or youth choir for nearly a year now plans to go on the upcoming choir mission trip. The student still is not attending choir, does not know the music, and has not participated in the fund-raising events. The parents are demanding (and even

threatening) that he be allowed to go on the trip. The young person's sibling has been a loyal member of the youth choir.

(6) My small group of auditioned/selected singers comprise an ensemble. They tackle difficult pieces and have done a great job. Because of the kind of literature we do, it takes a long time for the piece to mature and requires a tremendous commitment on the part of the group to rehearse. One group member does not show up for some of our rehearsals. He never lets us know he will be absent. I consider him an at-risk youth. He is angry at the world, and I know this group is important to him. However, his behavior is becoming contagious and is affecting our ability to carry out our mission as a group.

(7) We were planning to do a children's choir musical and auditioned for the main parts. I did not have many teachers/parents involved in the auditions. After the parts were publicized, a parent was angry that her daughter did not get the main part. She accused me of various faults, one being that I had "taken a bribe" from the father of the girl who got the part.

(8) I receive much affirmation from my congregation. However, the pastor frequently criticizes my work and character. Our music program seems to be a success. I have tried prayer and reasoning with the pastor for nearly a year, but his attitude has not improved. His work in the church is not going as well and some members are unhappy with him. It is almost as though he is jealous. What should I do?

(9) During a Wednesday-night choir practice to prepare for a traditional worship service, the pastor addresses the choir at the end of the rehearsal. He has recently returned from a seminar. He informs the choir that there will no longer be a choir. The minister of music will become the worship team leader. Choir members will be encouraged to audition for the praise and worship team. The pianist will no longer play a piano, but an electronic keyboard. The services of the organist will no longer be needed. Drums and guitars will be added. No hymns will be sung. The offering will take place at the end of the service, and a vocal contemporary song will replace the instrumental solo. Recorded contemporary music will replace the prelude and postlude. The new format will be implemented this coming Sunday. How do we react?

(10) It has become known that a member of the church staff is having an affair with a member of the congregation. Both individuals are married, but not to each other. The staff member is now very contrite. The church member involved is angry and attempting to justify the situation. What should I do?

(11) A church member has accused you of inappropriate behavior or called into question a decision you recently made. Some examples might include a crude comment, a wasteful use of church funds, an affair, molestation of a child (in this case the accusation might be made by a child), etc. Consider these situations from both the position of guilt and of innocence. How do you respond?

These situations represent only a few of the possibilities, and there are many variations on these stories. May God be with you as you serve, helping you to anticipate human nature—yours and that of the people with whom you work.

• ***Donald Clark Measels*** *is the Dean of Fine Arts at Carson-Newman College in Jefferson City, Tennessee, where he teaches church music.*